THE DA VINCI PRIMER
A Concise Guide to the Mystery of
Rennes-le-Château

THE DA VINCI PRIMER

A Concise Guide to the Mystery of
Rennes-le-Château

GAY ROBERTS

THE DA VINCI PRIMER—
A CONCISE GUIDE TO THE MYSTERY OF RENNES-LE-
CHATEAU

First Published 1995 as 'The Mystery of Rennes-le-Chateau'
Revised 2000

This revised paperback edition first published 2006

ISBN 1-904408-21-4

Printed and bound by Lightning Source

Layout, repro and typesetting by

BANK HOUSE BOOKS
PO Box 3
NEW ROMNEY
TN29 9WJ UK

CONTENTS

FOREWORD

THE DA VINCI CODE has caught the imagination of millions of readers world wide in just the same way that THE HOLY BLOOD AND THE HOLY GRAIL did nearly twenty-five years ago. What is even more fascinating is the fact that the Church apparently perceives it to be such a threat - far more so than I remember happening with THE HOLY BLOOD AND THE HOLY GRAIL or any of the other non-fiction books on this subject - that it issues all kinds warnings from both the Vatican and the pulpit against forming any kind of belief that strays from their strictly orthodox teachings. Consequently, not only has interest in the book soared but so has interest in their Church, especially the Roman Catholic organisation Opus Dei. So maybe this was a good move on their part. After all, it is a fact that nothing increases interest like the threat of censure.

Machiavellian recruitment tactics aside, the success of THE DA VINCI CODE is a phenomenon that is worth looking at. After all it was by no means the first book of fact or fiction to take this kind of subject as its theme. Since it appeared on the internet first of all, it could be that its success is the result of building up such a firm electronic following. However, many of the other books on this and associated subjects have also been traded and discussed on the net but they have not captured the public imagination to the same extent.

Disregarding the business and marketing structure behind it, maybe it is just a book whose time has come. Maybe it is the thriller aspect of it that captures the mood of the day. Of course, stating that so much of it is based on real organisations and artefacts probably contributes a great deal to its appeal. Possibly it conjures up a sense of quest that is missing from the cocooned muddle in which we live in the early twenty-first century.

It is interesting that what appears to worry various authorities is that people will think it really does describe reality. But this is surely no more so than Sir Arthur Conan Doyle did with Sherlock Holmes, for example. This detective also has a cult following but despite the grip maintained on the readers' imagination, I doubt if their sense of reality is affected, apart from their disappointment when they find that 22b Baker Street does not exist.

My own introduction to this Alice-in-Wonderland world of mirrors, conspiracy theories and wild imaginative ideas where nothing is as it seems and nothing is ever found - well, never the thing that you're looking for – came over fourteen years ago. Browsing in the library on a wet afternoon in January 1992, I was short of ideas for reading matter when a black cover with a red and white script caught my eye. It was **THE HOLY BLOOD & THE HOLY GRAIL** by Michael Baigent, Henry Lincoln and Richard Leigh. I remembered it coming out some ten years earlier in a blaze of publicity regarding some secret that would rock the Roman Catholic Church to its foundations and bring down civilisation as we knew it. However, not being one to buy into this kind of hype without a very good reason for parting with my hard earned cash, I had decided to give it a miss. Ten years on, civilisation was still in tact, the Roman Catholic Church was still in situ at the Vatican and it looked like I had made the right original decision. So, as the book was sitting there on the library shelf and would not cost me anything, I decided to give it a whirl.

In this book, after an extraordinary journey starting on a barren rocky outcrop in the Languedoc area of the south of France and progressing through the religious, political and art history of Europe we end up back in the little village from whence we started, most of us fully convinced, I am sure, that Jesus Christ, the icon of the Christian religion, contrary to the tradition taught by the Church of Rome, was married to Mary Magdalene and fathered a child. A child who left Jerusalem with her after the crucifixion, sailed across the Mediterranean to the south of France and started a family of his/her own, which was the origin of the Merovingian dynasty of Frankish kings; and that on the death of his first wife, one of the later of these kings, Dagobert II, made a second marriage to a Visigothic princess of this area of France known as the Razés, and had a child who was the ancestor of the kings of France as well as much of the royalty of Europe.

8

Baigent, Lincoln and Leigh were not the first to posit this idea of the marriage of Jesus and Mary Magdalene and a resulting family. It was previously given a great impetus by the discovery and translation of the Dead Sea Scrolls and the so-called Gnostic Gospels discovered at Nag Hammadi in Egypt in 1945, and popularised in a slim volume, **THE JESUS SCROLL,** by Donovan Joyce in 1975. They did however inspire a tremendous amount of research into it and all the related subjects. While the quality of all this research varies a great deal, some very interesting information has been unearthed. And it is the results of some of this research that underpin Dan Brown's novel **THE DA VINCI CODE.**

To my knowledge, Clive Prince and Lynn Picknett were the first to notice that the figure to the right of Jesus in Leonardo da Vinci's painting of *THE LAST SUPPER* was female, contrary to all accepted opinions both in the art world and the religious teachings, and they discussed it in **THE TEMPLAR REVELATION** in 1997. Indeed the 'orthodox' authorities in both these communities are still firmly of the opinion that the figure is male; and yet to almost anyone looking at the picture either with an open mind or with no preconceived expectations, the figure is quite obviously female. The facial features are finer, softer, rounder, totally feminine compared to those of all the other male figures at the table. The figure of Jesus has finer features than the apostles but his is still an obviously masculine appearance compared to the person next to him on his right. That it could be Mary Magdalene fits in with everything that has been revealed about their real relationship in the Gnostic gospels.

It is this relationship that is at the heart of **THE DA VINCI CODE** and the novel takes it forward with verve and imagination, as any good novel should. But it should always be remembered that it is a novel, it is fiction. The statement at the beginning of the novel that it is based on two real organisations is a bit misleading. While Opus Dei is very much a real organisation, the same cannot be said for the Priory of Sion. There was an Order of Mount Sion, inaugurated probably by Godfrey de Bouillon around 1099 during the period of the First Crusade, but there is no evidence that it evolved into the Priory of Sion in 1188 or was presided over by the list of illustrious grand masters as claimed by the documents in the so-called *Dossiers Secrets* in the National Library in Paris. There is not a shred of evidence authenticating those documents and it is virtually certain that the whole file was created as part of a surrealist joke on the part of two gentlemen by the names of Pierre Plantard and Philippe de Chérisey.

There is certainly no suggestion anywhere that it exists to protect the 'sacred feminine' as stated in chapters 23 and 28 of **THE DA VINCI CODE**. A bit of dramatic licence has been taken here, I think. If the Priory does exist in any form similar to its portrayal in *Les Dossiers Secrets*, it is to protect the male heir. The only importance of women is as mothers and wives of the legitimate king.

This is not to say that there is not or has never been a Priory of Sion; only that the Priory as described in *Les Dossiers Secrets* is a sham. A great deal of research has been done into this organisation over the past ten to fifteen years and the only priory that bears any resemblance to this description was set up in 1956 on the Franco-Swiss border on the lines of a boy scout group and was more or less disbanded not long after Pierre Plantard's resignation in 1984. It is possible of course that Pierre Plantard may have been involved in another more clandestine group. He had a strong affinity for movements of an extreme right wing, nationalist, catholic, monarchist nature. Maybe he created the Priory of Sion as it appears in *Les Dossiers Secrets* as a way of bringing his hopes and his sympathies to a wider public. After all, Gérard de Sède's answer when asked by Henry Lincoln why the decryption of the parchments had not been published in his book, **L'OR DE RENNES**, (*The Gold of Rennes* and the book in which Henry Lincoln originally came across the story of Abbé Saunière) was, "Because we thought it might interest someone like you to find it for yourself." (Introduction to **THE HOLY BLOOD AND THE HOLY GRAIL**, 1982)

Back to **THE DA VINCI CODE**. The relationship of the

novel to the mystery of Rennes-le-Château is that many of the important elements and features of the Rennes mystery, as it is known, are encoded in the novel.

Following now are just a few examples:

-       Jaques Saunière, the curator of the Louvre whose murder provides the novel with such a gruesome, dramatic beginning, takes his name from the 19th century priest of Rennes-le-Château, the discovery of whose tale of rags to unexplained riches was the start of the Rennes mystery. Abbé François-Bérenger Saunière is supposed to have become extraordinarily rich after finding something in his church during the course of its renovation. But no-one knows exactly what and that is what this book is devoted to - all the main elements that comprise the Rennes mystery.

-       Bézu Fache, the policeman pursuing our hero and heroine takes his first name from a village and château with templar associations not far from Rennes-le-Château. Le Bézu is a tiny village on the pilgrimage route to Saint James de Compostela in Spain. The château was thought for many years to be a Templar château and repository of their great wealth or great secret, although doubt has been cast on that idea in the last few years.

-       Robert Langdon's name bears a very close resemblance phonetically to the name of this area of France - the Languedoc. This phonic association is vital in the Rennes mystery which is full of puns, phonetics and word games.

-       The name Sophie, on the other hand, has the very straightforward meaning of wisdom – except that traditionally, although wisdom is personified by a beautiful woman, that woman is not young. She is beautiful because she is old with experience of life and she has achieved wisdom by learning from those experiences.

-      Sister Sandrine Bieil, the house manager of the church of Saint Sulpice in **THE DA VINCI CODE** shares her name with Abbé Bieil, the Director General of the seminary of Saint Sulpice to whom Saunière is said to have presented himself and the parchments when he stayed in Paris, and the uncle of Abbé Hoffet, who was said to have translated the parchments.

-      Inspector Jérôme Collot has an interesting name. It bears a striking resemblance to Collet, the company that published **MYTHOLOGIE DU TRÉSOR DE RENNES** (The Mythology of the Treasure of Rennes) by René Descadeillas, the highly respected curator of the library at Carcassonne, historian and researcher into the Rennes mystery from 1957 until his death in 1986. A member of the prestigious research organisation The Society for the Scientific Study of the Aude, he was a great sceptic of the Rennes mythology and few researchers carry the weight of his conclusions and opinions.

-      The 'lame saint' and the 'draconian devil' could be Saint Roche and the devil both of whom were wounded in the knee and statues of whom were placed in the church at Rennes-le-Château by Abbé Saunière. The Great Lame Devil of the Languedoc is a very well known character in the folklore of the area and was brought to life in the great romantic saga of Angélique in the 1950s and 60s by Sergeanne Golon.

-      It is said that initiates of many secret societies cluster around the Rennes mystery, using various elements for their own purposes. They work on the principle that those who have 'the eyes to see' will understand, and it is their custom to use certain signals for recognition purposes, one of the most notable being the reversed letter N. However, whichever society it is, they have not revealed themselves to Joe Public to date. The two best known appearances of the reversed N in the Rennes mystery are in the signature of the painter EM Signol in the church of Saint Sulpice and on a gravestone in the cemetery at Rennes-le-Château – no, these are not typographical errors. As regards **THE DA VINCI CODE**, it does of course appear in the title on the cover where the V and I of Vinci are run together.

\-   Finally, we come across Leigh Teabing, whose name is an anagram of Baigent and Leigh, two of the writers of **THE HOLY BLOOD AND THE HOLY GRAIL**, the book that started the whole interest in the mystery of Rennes-le-Château in the English-speaking world in 1982 and turned it into the global phenomena that it is today.

These are just a few of the examples connecting **THE DA VINCI CODE** with the Rennes mystery. There are many more which it will be much more fun and rewarding for you, dear reader, to discover for yourself by reading this book and many others from the vast bibliography in many languages that is available on this truly fascinating and absorbing subject.

GAY ROBERTS 2006

INTRODUCTION

Nestling on a hillside in a quiet corner of the Aude Valley in the Languedoc region of southern France close to the Pyrenean border lies the little village of Rennes-le-Château. Before the Great War of 1914 the population numbered about three hundred inhabitants, but the munitions factories, the fields of Flanders, the Great Depression and the Second World War all took their toll and by 1946 the population was down to a hundred and three. However, it is not for its declining numbers that Rennes-le-Château is remarkable. The mystery of Rennes-le-Château lies in its peculiar affinity with hidden gold. In 1892 its parish priest, Bérenger Saunière, is thought to have made a discovery that brought him the riches of Croesus. He was known as the '*curé aux milliards*' - the millionaire priest. His discovery is thought to have been related to something very old, although exactly what no-one knows, since he and his confidante went to the most extraordinary lengths to keep its nature a secret.

In trying to unearth the secret of his good fortune, researchers have discovered a web of connections that touches almost every major tradition of Western religion, philosophy and historical association, and at almost every turn we are confronted with the idea of gold. Sometimes it is actual gold as money and jewels. More often it is gold in the metaphorical sense - gold symbolising the glory and the curse of kings as in the story of Midas; gold as the power of knowledge and spiritual enlightenment; gold as alchemical transformation, turning what is base into what is pure.

Many of these connections are dubious at best, spurious if not actually fraudulent at worst. That is where sifting through the Rennes mystery is just like panning for gold. You shake through all the matter that comes your way and every now and then a lump of gold gleams through the dross. But it is not the details of the more obscure associations that concern us here. The committed Rennes hunter can pursue those at his or her leisure. This book is an attempt to chart a basic course through the myriad theories and associations giving a brief outline of the enigma and the main connections for the newcomer.

As editor of **THE RENNES-LE-CHÂTEAU OBSERVER**, one day I received a letter asking me for an 'idiot's guide' to the Rennes mystery. I realised then that what was needed was a simple (!) guide giving the central thread and setting out the main points that mystery seekers can then follow as they please. So, the first part of this book gives a general outline of the Rennes mystery; then the main features each have a section to themselves, with a brief description of what they are and why they are deemed relevant to Rennes-le-Château; finally there is a summary of what seem to be the most important angles.

So, bearing in mind what started this publication going, what better way to begin than with the 'IDIOT'S GUIDE.'

GOOD HUNTING!

THE 'IDIOT'S GUIDE' TO
THE MYSTERY OF
RENNES-LE-CHÂTEAU

Once upon a time there was a sleepy little village in the south of France called Rennes-le-Château. However, it had not always been so. Before history was documented, it was inhabited by megalithic man. It had also been a centre of the Celts, one of the most flamboyant and influential races the world has ever known. They wrote little down in a documented form that we can recognise and yet their influence still pervades as a source of language and cultural pride throughout Europe, particularly along the Atlantic seaboard.

Civilisations came and went, empires rose and fell, and under various names Rennes was a centre of imperial forces. Under the Romans it was called Rhedae. In the fifth century AD it was occupied by the immensely rich and powerful Visigoths of the Razés. They were allied by marriage to the Merovingians, the Frankish dynasty of priest-kings that the swept through France via Eastern Europe and the River Danube. In their various guises, possibly to the present day, they have persistently claimed the right to occupy the throne of France, should the opportunity to do so ever arise again.

Called Rhaede, it became a stronghold of the Knights Templar, whose political and economic power spread across the whole of Europe to the Holy Land for 200 years from the twelfth to the early fourteenth centuries AD. During this period it was the home of the Cathars, the Gnostic community slaughtered as heretics by the Church of Rome.

After the fall of the Templars, reverting to its old druid name of Rennes, it fell into sleepy obscurity until 1885 when a new parish priest named Bérenger Saunière arrived. During the course of renovating the little church of Rennes-le-Château (as distinct from the town a few miles away called Rennes-les-Bains), he found something that seems to have made him immensely rich. Despite all sorts of rumours and speculations, no one knows exactly what he found; but, from having to count every sou for a living, within a few months of his find he began to spend money on a grand scale. He built a tower called the Tour Magdala, a villa called Bethania, which he filled with fine objects of great worth and sumptuous furnishings, and a magnificent library. However, he never lived in it himself. He also constructed a road and put in a water system for the village. He did a few very odd things such as collecting stamps of no apparent worth and roaming the countryside collecting stones. To his parishioners' disquiet, he defaced gravestones in the cemetery and changed from being good-humoured and helpful to being arrogant, morose and solitary, his only companion being his housekeeper, Marie Denarnaud. Perhaps the strangest things he commissioned were a statue of Notre Dame of Lourdes placed on top of the Visigothic pillar that used to support the old altar in his church - on this pillar he carved the words PENITENCE! PENITENCE! and MISSION 1891 - and the decoration of his church. A statue of a devil, presumed to be Asmodeus, greets the visitor at the entrance, which bears two inscriptions - TERRIBILIS EST LOCUS ISTE (This is a fearful place) and PAR CE SIGNE TU LE VAINCRE (By this sign you will conquer him). The church, which is dedicated to St. Mary Magdalene, is rich in the symbolism of secret societies. The Stations of the Cross are each depicted with something out of place, implying a coded message, and they are placed in reverse order.

He became so rich that he even had his own banking official to attend to his affairs. He entertained lavishly and spent a prodigious amount on alcohol, especially on rum imported directly from Martinique. On the appointment of the new Bishop to the See of Carcassonne, he was summoned to account for his expenditure, which far exceeded his annual stipend of four-hundred-and-fifty francs. This he refused to do so. The bishop accused him of simony (trafficking in masses) and suspended him from office. Saunière appealed to the court at the Vatican, who would not hear him until he had talked to the bishop. This he consistently refused to do. So the Vatican although unable to find him guilty, had no choice but to uphold his suspension.

His last few years were spent largely alone, except for the company of Marie Denarnaud, and in failing health. The only journey he is known to have made outside his parish during this period was a pilgrimage to Lourdes in 1916. He suffered a stroke on 17th January, a significant date that crops up in many episodes to do with the Rennes mystery, and died five days later on 22nd January. After his death his body was draped in a table-cloth edged with red pom-poms and placed in an armchair in a downstairs room in the villa. During the day many people including all the women from the village came and paid their respects, each one plucking a pom-pom from the cloth and taking it away with them. He was buried two days later. When his will was read, he was found to be penniless; there was nothing left to bequeath. He had already transferred all his wealth and his secrets to Marie Denarnaud in a reciprocal will beforehand. She had been his friend and confidante for many years and although she also died penniless, she took the secret of his wealth with her to the grave thirty six years later almost to the day.

Tales, unsubstantiated to date, abound of him having visited Paris, meeting with people involved with all kinds of occult activities, including Emma Calvé, the most celebrated opera singer of the day, and of his purchase of copies of some paintings including *LES BERGERS D'ARCADIE* (The Shepherds of Arcadia) by Nicolas Poussin, the enigmatic 17th century painter, who was the father of the French Classical school of painting. However, although he did go there in 1913, the evidence of his invoices and diaries suggests that he did little more than have his photograph taken and restock his wine cellar. If he did meet any of the people he is supposed to have met or buy any of the paintings, either he did not mention them in his notebooks, or the documentary proof has gone missing.

Many important legends and traditions seem to touch the Rennes mystery. Mention a theme and someone somewhere will say that they have cast-iron proof that the key can be found at Rennes-le-Château. Speculation on the source of Saunière's wealth ranges from Alchemy to Zoroaster, the treasure of Blanche of Castille, the secret of the Cathars, the Holy Grail, the Turin Shroud, the Ark of the Covenant, the treasure from the Temple of Solomon, landscape geometry, prehistoric genetic engineering on mankind by visitors from Outer Space and the key to the End of the World - all have their advocates. Freemasonry is said to have its finger in the pie and with it a whole sporranful of Scottish connections, the most notable being the Sinclair family and the Stuarts, who are both said to have been connected by marriage with the original Merovingian princes and their medieval descendants, the houses of Anjou , Guise and Lorraine.

We have a hidden pope (a recent discovery so no details here yet), hidden kings, hidden temples, hidden tombs, hidden messages in the landscape, legendary hoards of hidden treasure, the Hidden Tradition itself.

Is there a solution to the Rennes mystery? I suppose that depends on the questions you ask. It is a cultural equivalent of the Cretan labyrinth. There are many blind alley ways on the way to the centre; and just as many on the way out. Which way do you want to go? This way or that? Which ever way it is, I cannot guarantee exactly what you will get out of it. But whatever it is, it will be interesting, absorbing and light-years more entertaining than watching television.

THE LEGACY OF BÉRENGER SAUNIÈRE

At the end of 1942, an industrial worker named Noël Corbu sent his children to a quiet corner of the Aude valley in the Languedoc area of southern France to escape the danger posed by the German occupation of their native town of Perpignan. Although they did not realise it then, this was the beginning of one of the biggest treasure hunts of modern times. The Corbus were so taken with the area that, after living in the village for four years, they eventually brought a property. This property had been the estate of a wealthy priest called Bérenger Saunière and the village was called Rennes-le-Château.

The current owner of the abbé's estate, which included a villa called Bethania and a tower called the Tour Magdala, was a diminutive old lady by the name of Marie Denarnaud, who had been the abbé's friend and confidante for many years until his death in January 1917. Although she was the sole beneficiary of his wealth, by April 1918 she was borrowing from friends to survive. Things went from bad to worse. By 1922 the tax inspector was asking questions about her finances. Many of the valuables that Saunière had bought for the villa had disappeared, thanks to numerous visitors with light fingers and few scruples, and to Marie's tendency to offer her creditors goods for lack of money. Thanks to the generosity of Saunière's old friends, she managed to get by, eventually scratching a living by selling chickens, rabbits and the produce from her kitchen garden.

As the abbé's friends grew older and died, her relationship with the village, which had been cool when he was alive, became warmer as she needed to turn to them more and more for support. However, she maintained a well-merited distrust of strangers, after having seen them denude the estate of most of its valuables, unable to stop the plunder. Her most memorable moment of this nature was seeing German soldiers during the 1939-45 war use the curtains to polish their boots. Although the estate had been for sale for nearly 30 years, so many prospective buyers had let her down. So it took nearly two years before she was willing to trust the Corbus enough to accept their offer.

In fact, not only did she sell it to the Corbus, she also lived with them as part of the family until her death in 1953. It was her stories of the abbé and that: "what he left would feed the whole of Rennes for a hundred years and still be some left over," and her comment that: "people here are walking on gold without realising it," that led to the modern resurgence of interest in Rennes-le-Château.

The secret of the abbé's wealth was known only to him and to Marie. When Noël Corbu was struggling to make ends meet in a business venture in Morocco in 1949, she did tell him not to worry and that one day she would tell him a secret that would make him a very rich man. But it was not to be. In 1952 her strength began to fail and she became senile. She hardly knew what she was talking about and she seemed to have lost interest in revealing her secret. She may even have forgotten it by then. In the third week of January 1953 she had a stroke that left her paralysed, blind and deaf and she died without recovering consciousness on 29th January.

After her death, during the process of sorting out her affairs, the Corbus gained access to her private room. There among her personal possessions were several boxes containing all kinds of notebooks, letters, invoices, and other documents all relating to the life of the abbé.

At this time, after the failure of his business in Morocco, Noël Corbu decided that the best way to make a go of things so that they could stay in Rennes-le-Château would be to turn the villa into a hotel-cum-restaurant. Opening on Easter Day in 1955, after a difficult start due to the inaccessibility of the village, their reputation grew by word of mouth and soon business was flourishing.

The success of a venture such as this depends upon the geniality and enterprise of its host, and Noël Corbu, being a genial and enterprising man, often used the story of the abbé to entertain his guests. Several regional journalists got to hear of it and they printed the story in their newspapers. Then, on 12th January 1956, *'La Dépêche du Midi'* published a major story called *'The famous discovery of the millionaire priest of*

Rennes-le-Château': "*From a hammer blow to a pillar supporting the main altar, Abbé Saunière discovered the treasure of Blanche of Castille,*" with one of the abbé's contemporaries swearing he saw chests full of ingots in a room in the château. Reprints of this article appeared in newspapers and magazines not just in France but in many other countries as well, and soon Rennes-le-Château was inundated with visitors, both celebrated and unknown, from all over the world.

Some came to find out more about the story. Some came to be seen and to say that they had been there. Many came actively looking for gold. Some of these amateur treasure hunters would stop at nothing in their quest for riches, sometimes employing the most bizarre methods of detection, such as seances, table-turning, pendulum power, radiesthesia and divination with cards. Eventually the first flush of treasure fever died down. Those who found nothing after their initial burst of enthusiasm went back home leaving a small core of dedicated researchers following, in the main, the slower but better tried and tested methods of documentary research combined with field trips.

One day Noël Corbu was walking by one of these excavations, which had involved some digging in the hotel grounds, when he noticed his dog playing with a bone. It was part of a skeleton, which was found to be, to his horror, one of three sets of human remains buried there relatively recently. After an enquiry, it was decided they were the remains of three young men, probably soldiers killed by the Resistance at the end of the last war. Another much older skeleton was discovered several years later. This one, dating from the eighth or ninth century, was found by the main door of the villa, hidden by a piece of pottery situated at the same level as the skull, which had been exposed, presumably unnoticed when the workmen were digging to install running water.

To cope with the hordes of visitors that now flooded the village and who, when visiting the villa, wanted to hear more about the millionaire priest and his treasure, Noël Corbu made a twenty minute tape-recording from which they could learn something of the geography and the history of the area, with its Druids, Visigoths, Templars, Cathars and with the main narrative devoted to the story of the Abbé Saunière. In essence, the tape goes as follows:-

"THE HISTORY OF RENNES-LE-CHÂTEAU is lost in the mists of time. Remains from prehistoric, Iberian, Gaulish, Roman and Romano-Gallic periods show that people have always lived in the area. Even before the Visigoths, Rennes-le-Château was a big city, probably the capital city of the Sociates, the tribe of Gauls that held Caesar at bay for a long time." Its strategic importance is obvious when he describes the main points on the landscape - Bugarach to the south-east, Cardou to the East, Becq and the Franges to the south, the River Aude meandering westwards and Rennes-le-Château looking north to Alet and Carcassonne.

"In the fifth century, as the capital of the Visigoths, it was called Rhaede and had a population of thirty thousand inhabitants. The citadel covered an area three times the size of the village itself. It was defended by the surrounding châteaux of Coustaussa, Blanchefort, Arques, Bézu, Caderonne, Couiza and the fortress of Castella.

"The Visigoths were Arians and were thus declared to be heretics by the Church of Rome; and Rhaede bore the full brunt of the infamous Albigensian crusade during the 13th century. At one point during this period, the territory of Rhaede seemed to have been sold to the King of Castille, who allowed the Spaniards to invade Septimania (the medieval name for this part of Languedoc) to recover their expenses. The resulting plunder left Rhaede in a state of ruin from which she never recovered. Her inhabitants left the plateau for better pastures and the once-great citadel shrank to become the tiny village of Rennes-le-Château slumbering away in peaceful obscurity until the arrival on 1st June 1885 of a new parish priest, Bérenger Saunière.

"For seven years Abbé Saunière lived the life of a poor country parson, getting by on his stipend of four-hundred-and-fifty francs a year. Then, in February 1892 while his tiny parish church, which had almost been in ruins when he arrived, was undergoing renovation, the workmen discovered a box containing some parchments in a pillar supporting the main altar. He stopped the work immediately and, it is said, he took a trip to Paris the very next day, although there is no confirmation of this.

"On his return, he had the workman carry on working in the church. However, he started digging in the cemetery by himself. He demolished the tomb of the Countess of Blanchefort and erased the inscription on her tombstone. The municipal council got wind that something was going on and forbade him to dig in the cemetery. But it was too late. He built walls around the garden and in another small garden, placed the Visigothic pillar from the old altar, which he defaced by carving MISSION 1891 on it, supporting a statue of Notre Dame of Lourdes. He then embarked on a massive programme of construction, which involved the complete restoration of the presbytery, the building of the Villa Bethania and the Tour Magdala, a ring road and a winter garden. The total cost in 1900 was one million francs, the equivalent in 1956 of two-hundred-and-fifty million francs. He bought sumptuous fittings and furnishings and began to live, and receive visitors, like a king. His consumption of alcohol was prodigious - seventy litres of rum a month plus all kinds of wines and spirits.

"When the Bishop of Carcassonne, Monsignor Billard, called to see him one day, he was surprised at Saunière's lifestyle, but he made no comment. His replacement, Monsignor Beauséjour, however, was of a more inquiring nature. He demanded that Saunière account for his income and that he should come to Carcassonne to do so. Saunière refused, saying he was too ill to leave. He sent a false certificate from Dr Rocher to prove it. In a letter to Saunière, Dr Rocher seems to have been happy to provide the false document. Too ill to go to Carcassonne, Abbé Saunière was not too ill to venture further afield in secret to Spain, Switzerland and Belgium. In reply to any written correspondence while he was away, Marie would send off bland, pre-written and signed notes giving the impression that he was at home and incapacitated.

"Getting no response from Abbé Saunière, Monsignor Beauséjour accused him of trafficking in masses and suspended him. Saunière refused to submit and engaged a lawyer, Canon Huguet, who went to Rome at Saunière's expense. The whole legal process lasted seven years, but ended in deadlock. The Vatican said it could not deal with Saunière's case until he had spoken with Monsignor Beauséjour. Saunière said he would speak only to Rome.

"During these years, Saunière finished the building work on his estate and he was planning more major works. He wanted to construct a road from Couiza to Rennes-le-Château to accommodate the motor car he was planning to buy. He had running water piped to the village, a chapel built in the cemetery and a rampart built all around Rennes-le-Château. He was planning to build a fifty-metre high tower with a circular staircase, at the top of which would be a magnificent library and an access to the tower from the winter garden. The total cost of these works would be eight million francs or two billion in today's (1956) money. On the fifth of January he accepted the estimate and signed for the work to begin. But on the twenty-second of January he caught a chill on the terrace and died of a heart attack complicated by cirrhosis of the liver.

"On his death, his body was placed in an armchair in the drawing room of the villa and draped with a cloth edged with red pom-poms. He was left there for the day during which time many people came and paid their respects by cutting off a pom-pom and taking it away with them. He was buried in a tomb which he had been building in the cemetery.

"The members of the Saunière family were all agog to find out who would inherit his wealth. But, to their consternation, there was nothing left. Everything was in Marie's name. The family received nothing.

"At Saunière's death, Marie underwent a complete change of behaviour. She withdrew to the presbytery and became a recluse, a model of austerity. She would not sell the estate, but, little by little, it fell into decay as valuables were filched by unscrupulous visitors. Finally, she decided to sell what was left to the Corbus, who, after her death, eventually changed the estate into the Hotel de la Tour."

According to an unpublished manuscript by Noël Corbu, Marie had a much more important role in the decipherment of the parchments that has been noted hitherto. Both she and Saunière tried to decipher them before he took them to Paris; it was she and her family who gave him the money for that trip; and it was she who found the gravestone with the key to the actual location of the treasure.

Apart from the two previous paragraphs, this was the basic structure of the narrative that was told until the 1960s, when events took a different turn.

THE FABLE OF ABBÉ SAUNIÈRE

In 1967 the book called **LE TRÉSOR MAUDIT** (The Accursed Treasure) by French author, Gérard de Sède, appeared. This was an entertaining, lightweight concoction based on the tale of Abbé Saunière, but filled out with some speculative embellishments to make it a good mystery read. So, according to this account, the secret he found in his Church consisted of four parchments, two of which are genealogies, and the other two being coded messages, one of which is so difficult to decipher that even modern computers could not break the code without the appropriate key. The decryption was not given by Gérard de Sède but, when decoded, the parchments contained the following messages:-

BERGERE PAS DE TENTATION QUE POUSSIN TENIERS GARDE LE CLEF PAX DCLXXXI PAR LA CROIX ET CE CHEVAL DE DIEU J'ACHEVE CE DAEMON GARDIEN A MIDI POMMES BLEUES

The usual translation of this, although not necessarily the most accurate one is:-

SHEPHERDESS NO TEMPTATION THAT POUSSIN TENIERS HOLD THE KEY PEACE 681 BY THE CROSS AND THE HORSE OF GOD I COMPLETE (OR I DESTROY) THIS DAEMON GUARDIAN AT MIDDAY BLUE APPLES

The second message with its usual translation is:-

A DAGOBERT II ET A SION EST CE TRESOR ET IL EST LA MORT

THIS TREASURE BELONGS TO DAGOBERT II KING AND TO SION AND HE IS THERE DEAD (IT IS DEATH is an alternative to the last phrase)

28

Having found these documents he is then said to have shown them to Mgr. Billard, who sent him to Paris at his expense, to the seminary of St. Sulpice. During his three-week stay he is also said to have met a number of celebrated ecclesiastics, artists and occultists including the famous opera singer, Emma Calvé with whom he is said to have formed a close and lasting friendship. While there, he is also supposed to have bought copies of three paintings LES BERGERS D'ARCADIE by Nicholas Poussin, THE TEMPTATION OF ST ANTONY by David Teniers and a portrait of POPE CELESTINE V by an unknown artist.

On his return to Rennes-le-Château, apparently he went to the cemetery and erased the inscription on the gravestone of Marie de Nègre d'Ables, Marquise de Blanchefort, not knowing that the inscription had been copied into a book called PIERRES GRAVÉS DU LANGUEDOC (Gravestones of the Languedoc) by one Ernst Stüblein. After this, he began to spend on an unprecedentedly lavish scale as detailed in the narrative by Noël Corbu. When Mgr. Beauséjour replaced Mgr. Billard, he called Saunière to account for his lifestyle, which he refused to do. Suspended by local tribunal for trafficking in masses, Abbé Saunière appealed to the Vatican, who, contrary to the Corbu account, and to his own papers, exonerated him and reinstated him. It also says that, despite being in perfect health, on 17th January, the feast day of St Anthony and of St Sulpice, and the date of the death of Marie de Nègre d'Ables, he suffered a sudden stroke, five days after Marie Denarnaud had ordered his coffin. The priest who was called to his bedside to hear his confession was said to have fled in horror, a broken man. His death and the curious preparations and ceremony that followed are as recounted by Noël Corbu.

This is the story that was taken up by Henry Lincoln, who, after doing a bit of research in the National Library in Paris, came across a batch of documents called Les Dossiers Secrets (the Secret Dossiers). These purported to give virtually the whole story of Abbé Saunière's wealth, linking it with the ancient Merovingian kings of France, said by historians to have died out in the middle of the eighth century AD, but claimed by these documents to have been perpetuated in secret by various noble families, and through the auspices of various groups and secret societies, such as the Order of the Knights Templar, and the Priory of Sion. It is in these Secret Dossiers that the interpretation of the parchments is given. But more of them later.

It was Henry Lincoln who, in the book THE HOLY BLOOD AND THE HOLY GRAIL (1982), made the jump from Saunière finding parchments relating to the history of France to Saunière finding documents proving that Jesus did not die celibate on the Cross but was married to Mary Magdalene, who came to the Languedoc (Southern Gaul and specifically Rennes-le-Château) with their child, who would be the ancestor of the Merovingian dynasty of kings. Of course in true story telling style, Henry Lincoln does not actually state this as fact but, by the time you get the end of the book, this is what the reader firmly believes has been proved.

REALITY OR FICTION?

It is important to emphasise that the events related in the fable section are just that – a fable. They have not been verified as fact as yet and, as far as is known, they were constructed as fiction purely for dramatic effect in Gérard de Sède's novel. And it is unlikely that the original intention of the novel was anything more than just that - a good mystery read using a factual base that had already appeared in a book by Robert Charroux, **TRÉSORS DU MONDE** (Treasures of the World) in 1964 after he too had visited Noël Corbu at the Hotel de la Tour.

Of course, almost nobody reports absolutely everything they do, and just because things are not recorded in the notebooks available, it does not mean that he did not do them or something similar, or that he was not involved in anything of this nature. Although they are fictionalised in Gérard de Sède's book, they may be based on known facts or well-founded rumour. Saunière and Marie were so keen to keep their secret absolutely to themselves that other evidence may have been destroyed before his death. Marie could have destroyed it later. If she was seen burning sheaves of papers after his death, it may have been notes referring to the secret, not old bank notes, as the legend would have it. If it was she who said they were banknotes, perhaps she was just saying so on Saunière's instructions, just as she sent out correspondence implying the abbé was sick when he went off on his jaunts.

At the time of writing this guide, there is still no proof that he ever went to Paris in the 1890s, that he ever met the people mentioned or that he ever bought copies of any paintings by Poussin, or Teniers, or anyone else, although evidence has recently come to light suggesting that he led a secret life in Lyon and belonged to a Martinist order there. His health may have improved slightly in the weeks before his death, but he was certainly not at his best before his final heart attacks. His confessor was not known to have suffered any mental trauma following administration of the Last Rites, and Saunière's suspension was not lifted until quite literally the moment of his death. The invoice for his coffin is dated 12th June, not 12th

January. No original pictures, tombstones, parchments, books by Ernst Stüblein or any other independent evidence has yet appeared in public to confirm any of the fable elements. All that can be said with any real certainty is that, according to his diary, in 1892 Bérenger Saunière discovered a tomb. He began spending money well before then, having received large amounts of money from the Chambord family, (the Chambords were claimants to the throne of France) after which his lifestyle changed from that of a poor country priest, having to count every sou in order to make ends meet, to that of the Lord of the manor, dispensing largesse as though he was born to it, and answerable only to the Pope.

Also, Marie was not quite as poor as has been alleged so far. She had enough money to pay for her niece's education. Maybe she made economies for herself so that she could do this.

Since most English speakers would have come to the mystery of Rennes-le-Château by way of the works written in English and available in this country, some of which consistently include these fictitious elements as though they were the facts, it is essential that newcomers are aware that not everything in these books, with their pages of footnotes and reams of bibliography and acknowledgements to seemingly impeccable sources, all implying years of meticulous and scholarly research, is necessarily true. Each book reflects the interest of the author and is inclined ultimately to give credence to their own pet theory. Later we shall look briefly at some of these authors and their works. But now, let us begin by considering what form the 'treasure' might have taken.

THE LEGEND OF THE DEVIL'S TREASURE

At the Château Blanchefort the Devil guarded a huge treasure. All the villagers knew it to be about 19½ million in gold. Mind you, whether it was gold sheep, gold cattle or gold pieces, no one knew exactly.

One day the Devil had time on his hands (before the Revolution, of course), so he decided to fill in a few idle moments by spreading his treasure out over the mountain. A pretty young shepherdess, seeing all the piles of shiny bright coins, ran home in excitement and called her family to come and see it. By the time they got there, the Devil had made it all disappear. But by now, the villagers' appetites were aroused. They agreed on a plan and went to see a wizard.

The wizard was no fool. If he succeeded in getting the treasure, he said, when they had it in their possession, he wanted half of it for his pains, and five hundred francs in advance for his journey. They agreed. Then he warned them that he was going to fight the Devil and that when he called, someone must come to his aid to defeat the Devil.

Readily they all agreed and went to their places. The wizard began to invoke the Devil with passes and threats, spells and incantations, tracing circles and strange figures on the ground. Suddenly there was a great noise. The villagers took fright and fled. The wizard called "Help me! Help me!" But to no avail.

A long time later he reappeared, unhappy, panting and covered in dust. "Where were you?" he said angrily. "I had the Devil at my mercy. If only you had come, we could have conquered him forever and the treasure would have been ours." The villagers were silent and shamefaced. "Cowards, the lot of you," said the wizard. "What a waste of effort! I'm going home." And pocketing his five hundred francs, smiling to himself as he turned his back on them, off he went to Limoux with one of the easiest sums he had ever earned.

M. de Fleury, the Lord of the villages of Montferrand, Bains and Rennes, as well as the Blanchefort ruins, was angry at the villagers for violating his land. But when he heard the story of the wizard and the imaginary millions, his anger abated and he forgave the villagers for their trespass, reckoning that they had learned their lesson. Not only had they no treasure, they were also out of pocket by five hundred francs.

THE MYSTERY OF RENNES-LE-CHÂTEAU lies in the nature of the treasure, if it exists at all, and the riddle it conceals. In general, the treasure can be considered to fall into one or more of three categories:-

1). Material treasure, i.e. gold, silver, jewels, etc.

2). Historical or political treasure - evidence of claims that would confer power on whoever can make a legitimate claim.

3). Spiritual or mystical treasure – the hardest to define, perhaps, but that which links mankind to an existence beyond the mundane.

There are several candidates for each of these categories and they are what we shall look at next.

MATERIAL TREASURE

There are five major sources of material treasure whose legendary hiding places are linked with Rennes-le-Château:-

1) Buried Treasure of the Visigoths
2) The Lost Treasure of Blanche of Castille
3) The Lost Treasure of the Templars
4) The Lost Treasure of Solomon, which could be the same as, or incorporated with the Lost Treasure of the Templars
5) The Lost Treasure of Jerusalem.

1) BURIED TREASURE OF THE VISIGOTHS

Along with the loot and plunder they gathered on their way from the Middle East to southern Gaul, the Visigoths acquired two priceless techniques, the secrets of which they guarded jealously, and the products of which made them fabulously rich. The first of these was the forging of blue steel, which produced a hard, flexible sword blade, far superior to the ordinary iron variety. At the time, the Goths were the only people who knew the details of this process. They were renowned for their metallurgy, probably inherited from their Celtic forebears. Since swords made from blue steel would have been prized more than rubies, they would have made their fortunes from them.

The other almost limitless source of their wealth was wine-making. When Constantine converted to Christianity in the fourth century, the wine trade received a very welcome boost. There was a massive demand for wine for use in monasteries and in church ceremonial, particularly in the countries of northern Europe that had no tradition of wine-making or wine-drinking. When the Visigoths came on the scene, they took to viticulture with great enthusiasm, and a flourishing trade was soon well underway. Thus, having plundered Rome of its treasure (which is reputed to have included that taken from the temple after the fall of Jerusalem) in 412 AD the Visigoths were now able to augment their wealth by means of legitimate trade.

Salt was in huge demand in ancient times, being both the main means of preserving food and an essential to life itself. Unless we maintain a healthy salt balance in our bodily fluids and tissues, we die. There is a mountain of salt, just over the border from Rennes in Spanish Catalonia, called Cardona, which made the fortunes of all its occupants, who became rich by chipping away at this natural resource. In the Aude Valley many place names attest to the erstwhile presence of salt deposits, such as the River Sals, the Salsigne mines and possibly Pech Cardou (the syllable 'Car' or 'Card' also indicates salt, as in Cardona on the Spanish side of the Pyrenees, near Barcelona). The name Saunière means salt box and there is a grave stone in Couiza commemorating the 'Saunière-Gabelle' family. The Gabelle was the infamous salt tax, the continued imposition of which was one of the causes of the outbreak of the French Revolution in 1789.

When Gothic princes died, they were buried with their wealth in the bed of a stream or a river. The flow of water would be diverted to allow the grave to be dug. After the burial, the water would then be allowed to pursue its natural course. This was a barrier to grave-robbing as the robber would have to know the exact location in order to divert the stream. As was the case with the Egyptians, there are tales of members of the burial parties being put to death afterwards, or of voluntarily committing suicide to prevent discovery or plunder, but these are difficult to verify. Like the Egyptians and many other pre-Christian cultures, the Visigoths believed they needed their grave goods for their sustenance in the afterworld. It is thought that Saunière may have discovered one of these burial sites and was making money by selling the treasure. He is known to have disposed of jewellery dating from that period. Was this the origin of Marie Denarnaud's comment that people were walking on gold without knowing it?

2) THE TREASURE OF QUEEN BLANCHE

In 1352 Blanche, Queen of Philippe le Cruel, King of Castille, escaped from her brutal husband who had thrust her from him and cast her into prison. Under the protection of the King of France, she took refuge at the nearby Château of Peyrepertuse, where she lived for five or six years. She spent a lot of time enjoying the hot springs at Rennes-les-Bains, which gave her relief from a skin condition, and she gave her name to the waters there known as the *'Bains de la Reine.'* With her she brought an immense treasure, which is thought to have belonged to the army, which was in rebellion against her brutal husband, with dreams of killing him. She is thought to have hidden the treasure in the area before her son-in-law, Henry Trastamare, came looking for her.

Noël Corbu tells of an earlier Blanche of Castille, mother of St Louis, and Queen Regent while he was still under age. She also had the royal treasury in her charge. During the Shepherds Revolt, when the vassals of France were attempting once again to reduce the power of the monarch, a strategy that included an attempt to abduct the young King (unsuccessfully, as he was saved by the citizens of Paris who came to his aid at the sound of the alarm bells), Blanche decided that Paris was too risky a place to keep the treasure. From here on history becomes speculation and, Rennes-le-Château being part of her property, she is said to have hidden it in a vault deep under the ancient citadel in two hundred chests and coffers. She used ten prisoners to help her, on the promise of their freedom. As they were stacking the chests, she had them walled in alive, no doubt to her mind giving them the freedom of eternal life. Using an inscription on a gravestone in the cemetery as the key, she wrote the access instructions on coded parchments, which she hid in the church in wooden rollers. Back in the land of verifiable facts, we know she then saw to the suppression of the revolt and died soon afterwards. The story continues that force of circumstance meant that no-one in the royal family knew how to find this treasure and it was not until six hundred years later, when abbé Saunière was having the church renovated that the instructions came to light.

Actually, it seems the treasure had been found before Saunière's time. In 1645 a shepherd called Ignace Paris fell down a hole while he was looking after his flock. He filled his beret with gold pieces that he said he had found at the bottom of the hole. Unfortunately the shock of his discovery caused him to lose his mind and he was killed trying to keep his gold safe. The lord of the manor and his men searched for the hole, but their efforts were in vain. It was not to be found again - unless it, or another entrance to the hoard was found by Saunière two-hundred-and-fifty years later. In 1956, when Noël Corbu was telling this tale, he estimated its value of about four thousand tonnes in weight, to be about four thousand million francs.

3) THE TREASURE OF THE TEMPLARS

One cannot examine the mystery of Rennes-le-Château without taking account of the Knights Templar. Arrogant, impetuous, mysterious, from apparently humble beginnings, the Knights Templar became the wealthiest, most formidable and most-feared fighting machine in Christendom from the twelfth to the fourteenth centuries. Their wealth was incalculable and as bankers and credit brokers to the mediaeval world, they also acquired immense political power. They were allied to kings and to the Church but independent of them, answerable only to the Pope. There are library shelves stacked with books about Templars that do far better justice to the history of the Order than there is room for in this little book. So this section merely sets out to examine what the source and the nature of their treasure might have been and its connection with the Rennes mystery.

Legend has it that, in 1118 AD, nine poor Knights led by Hugues de Payen and Godfrey de St Omer, vowing to live in poverty, chastity and obedience, formed an order dedicated to protecting the pilgrims' road to Jerusalem. Since they had no permanent place of residence, the King of Jerusalem, Baldwin II, granted them a temporary dwelling place in the stables of Solomon. However, as is often the case, the legend and the reality were somewhat different.

For one thing, there were certainly more than nine poor knights at the beginning. Nine very wealthy knights and their followers would be rather better equipped to do the work of protecting pilgrims from all the robbers and highwaymen on all the highways and byways leading from Europe to the Holy Land. According to the Patriarch of Antioch, more than thirty knights accompanied Hugues de Payen and the King gave them the house of Solomon for their residence along with several villages for their maintenance.

Evidence is also coming to light that it was Godfrey de Bouillon who was instrumental in setting up the organisation that would become the Knights Templar, some twenty years before their official inauguration, when he conquered Jerusalem in 1099.

Whatever the truth of their origins, their wealth and influence were indisputable and the original source of that wealth has been a matter of speculation ever since. They were rumoured to possess something which gave them not just wealth but great power as well. Since they spent a long time, probably several years, closeted in the stables of Solomon directly underneath the temple, before making any arrangements to protect the pilgrims, it is logical to assume that they were looking for something, and even that they may have found it. Since they were looking in his temple, they were probably looking for Solomon's treasure, i.e. The Ark of the Covenant. If they did find it, they would have needed a very secure place to keep it.

In 1306 Philippe le Bel took refuge from a rebellious mob in the Paris temple. This was a source of great embarrassment for him. He hated the Templars for their arrogance and disdain, for their closet support for the Cathars, and for their growing accord with the Arab world. But most of all, he hated them for their wealth, which he coveted, while he had to make do with false money. By stealth, intrigue and ruthless plotting, at dawn on Friday 13th October 1307, he had every Templar in France arrested at the same moment, their preceptories sequestrated and their goods confiscated. With the advantage of surprise nothing should have stood in the way of him gaining his objective. However, someone let the word slip and Philippe profited very little from his efforts. The treasure and the documents had disappeared. More significantly, so had the

Templar fleet. Rumour had it that the treasure was taken by wagon in the company of Templar treasurer, Hugues de Peraud, and loaded onto eighteen galleys at La Rochelle, from whence it sailed, with a surviving contingent of eighteen knights, never to be seen again. However, during the last ten years, research has tracked its possible destination to a small island in Scotland.

According to abbé Mazières, the Templars acquired their original wealth from managing all the country's mills. This brought them enormous riches and enabled them to contemplate a secret but cherished plan to set up their own independent state of the Midi, or Southern State, to include Aragon in Spain and Provence, the Roussillon and the Languedoc in Southern France. It was to be directed from their commanderie at Mas-Deu, near Perpignan. In reality, this threat to the authority of the King of France, Philippe le Bel, was probably far more crucial to his decision to have the order wiped out than an understandable desire to get his hands on their wealth, which common sense would have told him would not be likely to be kept all in one place in the Paris Temple.

What does all this have to do with Rennes-le-Château? On Friday 13th October 1307, the Templars of nearby Le Bézu were the only ones not to be arrested. The commander was a relative of the Pope, whose mother was one Ida Blanchefort. In 1156, Bertrand de Blanchefort, whose ancestral château lay only a few miles away, had brought German miners into the area, with strict instructions not to fraternise with the local populace, to work gold mines that had been exhausted when the Romans came into the area. Four centuries later, another engineer, César Arcon, studied their reports and concluded that, far from mining, they may have been smelting or creating some kind of underground depository. Incidentally, this is not the Bertrand de Blanchefort who became Grand Master of the Temple in 1153. That Bertrand de Blanchefort came from the Gironde.

There was a major preceptory a few miles way at Campagne-sur-Aude, and the Roussillon Templars were also invited to maintain the security of the region of Le Bézu. Local tradition says that they came to spy and to watch over a treasure of some sort. So, although the details are not known, what is surmised is that the Templars discovered something of great value in the Holy Land, which they removed from its original location and concealed at Rennes-le-Château.

4) THE TREASURE OF SOLOMON

Apart from his incomparable wisdom and his love for the Queen of Sheba, Solomon's main claim to fame is that he had the Temple built in Jerusalem to house all the sacred objects of the Hebrews, most especially the Ark of the Covenant. Now, either he was making a great show of his wealth, or rather the wealth that he had inherited from David, or the Ark contained something of great power as well as wealth. The remarkable thing about the temple was that, not only were the sacred objects themselves gold, but so much of the structure inside and out was either gold-plated or made of solid gold. Gold as a metal has two intrinsic qualities: 1) it is untarnished by air and water and 2) it can easily be beaten into shape. Although it can be alloyed with various metals, most chemical compounds are unstable and reduce easily to the pure metal. In other words, it is an excellent containment metal. This begs the question, 'What did Solomon have to contain?' particularly in the Ark itself; and is this what the Templars were looking for in the stables of Solomon, situated directly under the Temple itself?

Without proper protection the Ark had a devastating effect on everyone who handled it, as the Philistines found to their cost when they captured it from the Hebrews and took it back to Ashdod. Its effects were only neutralised when it was taken to 'the Field of Joshua. . . where there was a great stone' (Samuel VI 3-14). This is one indication that connects the Rennes mystery to sacred landscape geometry, which is discussed further on in this book. This also makes it the kind of treasure that would confer the power, as well as the wealth hinted at in a letter from abbé Louis Fouquet to his brother,

Nicolas Fouquet, superintendent of Finances to Louis XIV (the Sun King), and the wealthiest man in France.

5) THE LOST TREASURE OF JERUSALEM

After Alaric the Goth had sacked Rome in 410 AD he brought with him to his stronghold of Toulouse in southern Gaul the treasure of the temple at Jerusalem acquired by Titus in 70 AD. This included the table and the great seven-branched chandelier known as the Menorah, both made of solid gold, both to be held in the citadel at Carcassonne. In 507 AD the treasures of Toulouse fell into the hands of the Franks - all but the most important part, which Theoderic took to Ravenne. However, legend has it that the table and the Menorah were thrown into the Great Well of Carcassonne to escape the clutches of Attila. Another legend says that Alaric built seven towers, including the Tower of the Treasure to house it, although in reality this tower was built later by Philip the Brave. This tale comes from one Firmin Jaffus, who was not an historian but a professor of literature. The inhabitants of Carcassonne were fond of this legend and liked to believe that they sat on hoards of treasure and also on an intricate network of tunnels. While he was a librarian at the Municipal Library of Carcassonne in the mid-nineteenth century Jaffus wrote it down in a booklet called **THE CITY OF CARCASSONNE AND THE TREASURE OF THE VISIGOTHS**.

It seems that Gérard de Sède took over this legend, suggesting that the treasure was hidden not at Carcassonne but at Rhedae.

HISTORICAL AND POLITICAL TREASURE

In 1216 Simon de Montfort gave the Rhedae to one of his lieutenants, Pierre de Voisins. His son, also called Pierre, built the château as it is today. The Voisins were succeeded by the Marquefaves, who were succeeded in turn in 1422 by the d'Hautpoul-Aussillons, who stayed there until 1820. The Lords of Rennes were thought to be privy to a secret, which they guarded but did not own. Each Lord, from Pierre de Voisin, passed it on to his successor right down, it is assumed, to the last of the line, Elizabeth d'Hautpoul, Mademoiselle de Rennes. There has been endless speculation as to what the nature of this secret might be. There may have been details in the 1644 'will of great significance' that disappeared around that time. It is possible that Saunière found the will and discovered the secret guarded so closely by the Lords of Rennes.

If it was of historical or political interest, it is thought that it might provide proof, perhaps in the form of a genealogy or testament of some sort, revealing a legitimate claimant to the throne of France, should the opportunity to take it ever arise again. The number one lineage involved in this theory is that of the Merovingians

1) THE MEROVINGIANS

The origin of the Merovingians is as extravagant as any royal line. They claimed descent from ancient Troy, ancient Israel and the Arcadian throne of ancient Greece. Their ancestor, Merovée, was said to have had two fathers, one mortal and one mythical - a sea creature called a Quinotaur (although this name suggests five head of cattle rather than a sea beast). One feature that marked the Merovingians dynasty out from all the rest is that their kings were born to the position. They did not need to be crowned or anointed. On his twelfth birthday, the next one in line became heir to the throne automatically. They were the long-haired monarchs whose hair was never cut because of magical properties it was supposed to possess. They were priest-kings who conferred sacredness in their blood. This sacredness was not diluted by concupiscence with commoners. So long as one parent was a Merovingian, any child born of the union was equal to all Merovingians. Union sanctified and strengthened the blood tie rather than weakening it.

The Merovingian king that has been most associated with the Rennes mystery is Dagobert II, whose name appears in one of the coded parchments. He was a Hidden King. The Merovingian dynasty ruled both the kingdoms of the Franks - Neustria being France to the west with Paris as its capital, and Austrasia being France to the east with its capital at Metz in what is now Lorraine. However, the monarchs were weak, puppet kings. Real power lay in the hands of the Mayor of Palace, a sort of unelected prime minister. There was constant plotting and intriguing for power both within the kingdoms and between them.

Dagobert II inherited the throne of Austrasia at five years old, on the death of his father in 656. However, in order to get his own son Childebert, on the throne, the Austrasian Mayor of the Palace, Grimoald, persuaded him treacherously, over a five-year period, to go into voluntary exile for his own safety and that of the country. So in 661, after Grimoald had had his hair shorn, Dagobert went to Ireland in the care of Didon, Bishop of Poitiers. No force was used. The kingdom hardly felt a thing. The throne of Austrasia was legitimately vacant. Grimoald installed Childebert on the throne he coveted so much.

The Neustrians, however, had other plans. Biding their time, a year later they enticed Grimoald and Childebert to Paris where they were both imprisoned and put to death in 662. Ebroïn, mayor of the Neustrian Palace, now emerged as the brains behind, and the main beneficiary of, this manoeuvre. With the support of a Neustrian faction in the Austrasian court, he had his own son, Chilperic, married to Dagobert's sister, Blisschilde. Thus the usurper-king became brother-in-law to the king in exile. But Chilperic was not destined to die of natural causes. In 675 he was assassinated while out hunting and his wife and son (also called Dagobert) met the same fate. Dagobert II and his mother were the only members left of his branch of the family. Queen Himnechilde called him back from Ireland and he (or someone who claimed to be him) took the throne back in 676. All that is known of this period of his reign is that the two kingdoms fell into a civil war from which Austrasia emerged victorious, and that Dagobert was assassinated by his godson, Jean, in the sacred forest of Woëvres near the royal palace of Stenay, on 23rd December 679. This was a ritual killing, like that of William Rufus in England some four hundred years later. One document, the Vita Arbogasti, attributes to him a single son, who died before him in 678, and four daughters, who would not inherit directly.

As to the tales of his alliance by marriage with Gisela, the Visigothic princess of the Razés, the ceremony taking place in the Church of St Mary Magdalene at Rennes-le-Château, and his son, Sigebert, disappearing into the countryside of the Razés - all this makes a very good story, but readers should note that this version of the life and loves of Dagobert II comes from the DOSSIER SECRETS, a file of very dubious pedigree, all the documents of which were deposited in the Bibliothèque Nationale in Paris in the 1950s and 60s, and not one of which is an authentic original of the period from which they claim to date

Officially, since only males could inherit the throne, the Merovingian dynasty died out in the eighth century. But, bearing in mind the status of Merovingian unions, unofficially it is almost unthinkable that there were no Merovingian descendants anywhere on either the legitimate or the illegitimate side of the blanket. Maybe this is what underlies the mystery of Rennes-le-Château.

2) THE HOUSE OF DAVID & THE TRIBE OF BENJAMIN

Perhaps the most contentious theory of this nature is that the secret provides documentary proof that the story on which Christianity rests is not what it seems; that the reality of the events in Jerusalem nearly two thousand years ago was that Jesus, born of the Royal House of David and King of the Jews, made a bid for the throne of Israel and failed. However, to appease all sides, his crucifixion was faked to satisfy Rome, who crucified insurrectionists but did not want a full-scale riot, and to fulfil the prophecy of a Messiah in Jeremiah and other books of the Old Testament. He was rescued, drugged, but alive, to satisfy his followers and from there he escaped with his family, ending up by a circuitous route in southern Gaul. As a legitimate claimant to the throne of Israel, he would have been married at fourteen with descendants of his own by the age of thirty.

Mary Magdalene, who has a section to herself further on in this book, is the strongest candidate for his wife, and it could have been information relating to her that was kept secret by the Lord of Rennes. The church there has been dedicated to her in one way or another since at least the days of Dagobert II. Saunière has pictures and statues of her all over his church. Although no certain proof can be offered, it is a very strong possibility that both Mary Magdalene and the Merovingians were descended from the biblical tribe of Benjamin.

Benjamin was the youngest and best-beloved of Jacob's twelve sons, who formed the twelve tribes of Israel. The Benjamites were virtually exterminated as a tribe when they refused to kill some worshippers of Belial (a form of the Babylonian Goddess Ishtar and the Phoenician Astarte) who assaulted a Levite travelling through Benjamite territory, and ravished his concubine. Fleeing westwards, as the tribe was broken up, it is surmised that one of them may have joined the Arcadians in ancient Greece and this is the origin of the connections of the Merovingian tradition. Not wishing to wipe out a whole tribe, the elders of the other tribes eventually devised a plan whereby the Benjamites could find wives from the other tribes of Israel. This is where Mary Magdalene's Benjamite connection may have been formed.

Finally, though the source is once again one of those dubious Priory documents, so the information must be treated with the utmost caution, it is worth mentioning that, although the church at Rennes-le-Château is dedicated to Saint Mary Magdalene, it is said to be named after Magdala, the grand-daughter of Dagobert II.

3) THE ROYAL LINE OF KINGS

The Merovingian kings claim to be descended from the royal houses of Troy and Arcadia in the Pagan world and from Noah and the biblical tribe of Benjamin. Since their disappearance as a dynasty after the death of Childeric III in 754, it is claimed that their blood line has continued through the various royal families of Europe by means of inter-marriages. Lorraine, called Austrasia in the times of the Visigoths, was the power base of the Merovingians, and the House of Lorraine is thought to be the family through which the line of kings descends by marrying into the regal families of the moment, thus ensuring and strengthening their chances of survival. These families have included the Houses of Anjou, Plantagenet, Guise, St. Clair and the Scottish Houses of Sinclair and Stuart, and the current holder of the title, the Austrian Hapsburg-Lorraine. A member of this family who called himself Jean Orth when he wanted to travel incognito, visited Saunière at the Villa Bethania, but the reason for his visit is unknown. Another member of the family visited the Aude in 1975 and talked to a number of people interested in the Saunière affair. Apparently he said that the Saunière affair was known to the family.

There are many branches that claim various thrones. In the nineteenth century the church and the monarchy were fighting for their very existence against each other and against the Republican state. Each of the claimants had its own catholic support group. This way, the Church was sure to be on the winning side. Below are two known to be associated with the mystery of Rennes-le-Château.

THE SACRED HEART

Perhaps the biggest of these groups was the Sacred Heart,

which supported the claim of the Bourbon prince, Henry V, Count of Chambord. After half a century of squabbling for the throne and parliamentary changes of allegiance, in 1850 a chamber was elected with five hundred monarchist deputies. They offered Chambord the throne on condition that he kept the tricolour flag and held a plebiscite. Over the course of the next thirty three years Chambord refused three times, his reason being that he could only accept the position if the tricolour was replaced with the traditional white flag. In other words the Republic must foreswear its position. This was a very clever move by the Republicans, in fact. By their offering the claimant the throne, the monarchists were appeased. By offering it on terms the claimant could not accept – the seat without the power (absolute monarchical power was signified by the white flag, the power of the republic by the tricolor) – meant the republicans got what they wanted – a state without a monarch at its head. Thus the Count of Chambord died without gaining the throne.

The Sacred Heart movement was inaugurated in 1871at the instigation of Rohault de Fleury. He was a member of the same family as Paul-Urbain de Fleury, who, by his marriage to Gabrielle d'Hautpoul, was the Lord of Blanchefort and lord of the manor at Rennes-les-Bains. Essentially the movement believed that the rifts in France would never be healed until the whole country dedicated itself to the Sacred Heart of Jesus as personified by the legitimate monarch. So they consecrated the whole nation to this organ at Paray-le-Monial on 29th June 1871. They took their cue for this from the seventeenth century nun, Sister Marguerite Mary Alacoque, who had had a vision of Jesus approaching her with his heart open and bleeding and making that statement. The Basilica of Sacré Coeur in Paris was the ultimate expression of their aspirations, and the image of their movement – Christ, and other sacred figures such as the Virgin Mary, depicted with an open, sometimes flaming heart – can be seen in all its vivid glory in churches all over the Aude valley. Sometimes just the heart itself is depicted, girdled in flames. Abbé Saunière had some stained glass windows bearing this motif installed in the Villa Bethania.

HIÉRON DU VAL D'OR

Another contender for the throne during this period was a Monsieur Naundorff. A humble clockmaker by profession, he claimed to have one of the most illustrious and tragic ancestors of all. When Louis XVI and Marie Antoinette were executed in 1793, there was said to be a child of theirs in the Temple where they had been imprisoned who survived. Karl Naundorff claimed that he was a direct descendant of that child, and there were many supporters of that claim, including a very well-known character in the Rennes mystery – Emma Calvé. The Naundorff supporters were interested in a catholic revival but of a cultural not a religious nature. There was an esoteric tinge to their beliefs and they included a large number of very influential people in the Parisian occult fraternities. They were backed by a very obscure order known as the *Hiéron du Val d'Or*, (the Sacred Order of the Golden Valley).

This was a millennial sect whose purpose was

(a) to show that the origins of Christianity can be traced back to Atlantis via Judaism, the Egyptian religion, Judaism, etc,
(b) to reconstruct the sacred traditions of Gnosticism, Hermeneutics, Christian Cabbala, etc,
(c) to announce and prepare for the political and social reign of Christ the King in the year 2,000, and
(d) to teach the sacred name of AOR-AGNI, the key to all knowledge. From AOR-AGNI we get all kinds derivatives such as gold, light, fire, lamb and blood – all recognisable as symbols in Christianity as well as other religions.

However, in 2001, the Naundorffists hopes were dashed when DNA testing proved conclusively that Karl Naundorff was not of the blood.

Quite what this has to do with Rennes-le-Château and Abbé Saunière is unclear as yet, except that a page from one of their journals, dated 24th June 1926, describing all this is included in the Priory documents.

SPIRITUAL AND MYSTICAL TREASURE

There are three major candidates for this kind of treasure:

1) The Treasure of the Cathars
2) The Holy Grail
3) Mary Magdalene

1) GNOSTICISM & THE TREASURE OF THE CATHARS

In mediaeval Europe the Church of Rome was not the secure, established ecclesiastical authority it is today. In fact its position was so precarious that in 1208-9, it embarked on a policy of genocide against the Cathars of the Languedoc, unparalleled in Europe until the twentieth century. The policy of the Church towards the heretics and unbelievers, who were the unfortunate quarry of the crusaders, can be summed up in a single sentence supposedly uttered by one of the lieutenants of commander Simon de Montfort. When asked by the crusaders how they could tell the difference between Catholics and Cathars, as they were about to embark on the slaughter at Toulouse and Carcassonne, he is supposed to have said, "Kill them all. God will recognise his own."

In their beliefs the Cathars were dualists. They believed that underlying all existence was a universal conflict between two fundamental principles, GOOD and EVIL, locked in an eternal battle, part of which is for the soul of Man encased in his body. These principles are variously described as LIGHT and DARK, POSITIVE and NEGATIVE, SPIRIT and MATTER. God is the essence behind all creation and, as he is the FATHER OF ALL, his is the spirit world. He has an elder son called SATAN, who created the visible world, which is evil, and a younger son CHRIST, MICHAEL or JESUS, who is the LOGOS, the WORD sent in semblance of human form to save, through his baptism with the Holy Spirit and with Fire, that which was lost during Satan's reign (Satan also

51

being the God of the Old Testament). Later, the principles of one supreme God being the father of two sons, one good and one evil, developed into two supreme Gods, one good and one evil, in continual conflict. LUCIFER was the son of the Evil God, whose attack on the Heaven of the Good God caused the fall of the angels. The mission of the angel called CHRIST was to free them from imprisonment in their human bodies. This duel of two supreme Gods was at the root of the Cathar beliefs.

The Gnosis is that those who know, understand and have the wisdom, i.e. have been initiated into the secrets of duality, will teach it to those who are ready to receive it. This was an egalitarian religion. Women held equal rank and could become 'perfecti' and teachers on the same level as men. All were equal in the eyes of the Good God. Their message was contained in the New Testament, particularly in the sayings of Jesus, the Lord's Prayer and the Gospel of St. John. The paradox was that the daily life of the Cathars was closer to that advocated by Jesus than was that of the Church of Rome.

The Catholic Church treated heresy as an infection. Heretics were not people, they were agents of disease and should be purged wherever possible, Fire being the great religious antibiotic. As with the philosophy behind many a medical treatment, 'if it isn't hurting, it isn't working,' so the most brutal tortures were devised often by men of the highest moral convictions. What is extraordinary is that tens of thousands, maybe hundreds of thousands of men, women and children were sufficiently sure of their spiritual future that they were prepared to endure these tortures rather than renounce their faith. They sincerely believed that this was their route to everlasting life and they sincerely believed in that everlasting life.

In 1209 Pope Innocent II launched the Albigensian crusade. The Cathars' final stand in the Languedoc came in 1244 at Montségur, the impregnable castle high on a plateau where they held out for nine months. But, as the situation became untenable, the 'faidits' defenders were given amnesty and a safe passage away from the castle after confession to the

Inquisition. The remaining two hundred or so perfecti chose to be burned to death in the 'Field of Cremation' at the foot of the mountain. The night before the Cremation, according to tradition, three or four of the perfecti escaped with the Cathars' most treasured possession. There is no indication as to what it might have been, except that it must have been fairly lightweight and of little material value. From there it disappeared and has not been heard of in public since. One of the perfecti who escaped with the treasure was a man called Aniort, whose lands were eventually co-owned by Marie de Nègre d'Ables, the d'Hautpoul family and the Cazemajou, of whose estate Saunière's father was a manager.

2) THE HOLY GRA I L

'There is a thing called the Grail,' which is so precious it is guarded by a family of the noblest of men and the most beautiful of women, all of whom are pure in heart. It has the gift of bestowing on the supplicant all that is needed for their sustenance, all that their heart desires. It is the Cornucopia, the Horn of Plenty.

One of the most enigmatic artefacts to be associated with the Rennes mystery is the Holy Grail. The Grail legend goes as follows: Perceval, son of a Widowed Lady, leaves his home to become a knight. Having no courtly refinements, in his quest for adventure, he rides roughshod over everyone including various ladies, whose help he needs but leaves hurt and disappointed, gaining much experience but little wisdom. Eventually he comes across the maimed Fisher King, who offers him refuge for the night. During the evening the Grail appears, carried by a beautiful damsel. It is gold and studded with jewels. On seeing it, Perceval is supposed to ask a question. But, having learned little on his journey so far, he fails to do so and in the morning he wakes up to an empty, blighted landscape.

The question he should have asked was 'Whom does the Grail serve?' In other words, 'In whose service is the Grail?' or 'In whose service is the person who serves the Grail?' This

question is full of meaning in Celtic culture. When the Great
God Bran was decapitated, his head became a source of plenty
for many years. On its journey to London it sang and
prophesied for eighty years. While it remains buried under the
White Tower, facing France, Britain will stand. If it is
removed, as signified by the ravens leaving the Tower of
London, Britain will fall. If Perceval had asked the right
question, the king would have been healed and the land would
have been restored to fertility.

In Europe the legend was first recorded by Chrêtien de
Troyes, who was a well-known troubadour associated with
Marie de Champagne and the Courts of Love, for whom he
wrote the main body of his work. However, he wrote **LE
ROMAN DE PERCEVAL** or **LE CONTE DE GRAAL**
(The Romance of Perceval or the Story of the Grail) for
Philippe of Alsace. Unfortunately, due to his death in 1188, it
was left unfinished. However, after his death several more
versions appeared, embellishing and elaborating on the basic
legend. Robert de Boron produced a Christianised version in
1190 in which the Grail becomes the cup of the Last Supper,
taken by Joseph of Arimathea, who filled it with Christ's
blood when he was taken down from the Cross. Now the Grail
has become holy and acquired magic, healing properties.
Joseph's family became the keepers of the Grail, which is
brought back to England by his brother, Brons, who in his
turn becomes the Fisher King; and Galahad, who achieves the
quest for the Grail, is Joseph's son. Thus the Grail is said to
enter Britain's mythology during the lifetime of Joseph of
Arimathea.

Chrêtien's story is set in the age of Arthur, whenever that
may be. The Arthurian connection was reinforced by another
version appearing at this time called the **PERLESVAUX** by
an author who is unknown but, from the narrative content, is
thought to have Templar connections. Once again the blood
line is stressed with Perceval said to be of the lineage of
Joseph of Arimathea. The Christian element also appears in
the **PERLESVAUX** with Sir Gawain being cautioned that
whoever is made privy to the secrets of the Grail must himself

keep the secret safe. In the **PERLESVAUX** the Grail is something quite different from the two previous legends. Gawain sees it as a set of changing images, each accompanied by a fragrance and a great light. So the Grail here would seem to be a mental or a mystical experience rather than the physical gratification of Robert de Boron and Chrêtien de Troyes.

The most influential Grail romance, however, to appear at this time was **PARSIFAL** by Wolfram von Eschenbach, a Bavarian knight, who said he got it from Kyot of Provence, who was living in Toledo and who got it in his turn from a heathen by the name of Flegetanis. Flegetanis was said to be descended from Solomon and was a learned scholar of nature and astrology. 'He said there was a thing called the Grail, whose name he had read clearly in the constellations. A host of angels left it here on the earth.'

'Since then, baptised men have had the task of guarding it with such chaste discipline that those who are called to the service of the Grail are always noble men.'

Wolfram von Eschenbach's Grail is .' . .*a stone of purest kind. . .called lapis exilis. By the power of that stone the phoenix burns to ashes but the ashes give her life again. . . Such power does the stone give a man that flesh and bones are at once made young again. That stone is called the Grail.'*

Its guardians are called to it by their names, which appear with their lineage around the edge of the stone as the time for their appointed journey draws nigh. The Grail castle is called Munsalvaesche, which is thought traditionally to be the legendary Cathar castle of Montsalvat, which itself is identified with Montségur. The most important members of the Grail family are the damsel, Repanse de Schoye (Chosen Response), who is the Grail keeper, and Anfortas, the maimed king who cannot die until Perceval, who is his nephew, lifts the curse and in his turn becomes heir to the castle. The Arthurian connection is maintained with Perceval coming from Wales, but Arthur's court is set in France with Camelot located at what is now Nantes in Brittany.

While female members of the Grail family may make their origins known when they marry outside the family, males must keep theirs secret. If strangers ask for their pedigree, they forfeit their status as Grail guardians. This was Lohengrin's dilemma in Wagner's opera.

The most well-known of the later versions of the legend stem from Sir Thomas Malory's **LA MORTE D'ARTHUR**. In this version it is Lancelot who fathers Galahad, having been seduced by Elaine into thinking that she was Guinevere. Despite being considered the best knight in Christendom, he is not pure enough to achieve the Grail himself because, although Elaine was deceiving him, he genuinely thought he was making love to the Queen and thus he betrayed the King.

In summary, there are various interpretations of what the Grail might comprise:- 1) a Chalice; 2) a Stone; 3) a Hallucinogenic Medium; 4) a Thing of Gold studded with Gems; 5) a Platter; 6) a Head or a Skull; 7) a Lineage; 8) Mary Magdalene, who is the next subject for discussion.

The connection of the Grail with Rennes-le-Château is that the Lords of Rennes are known to have been the guardians of a secret since the days of the Templars and the Cathars, if not before. The nature of this secret has never been divulged to the outside world, although it is thought that a 'will of great importance' to the d'Hautpoul family, the last Lords of Rennes, which disappeared around 1644, may have provided a clue, since the Grail legends originated from this area of France and Spain. It has been surmised that the Grail and the secret kept by the Lords of Rennes may be associated if not actually one and the same thing.

3) MARY MAGDALENE

The church at Rennes-le-Château was dedicated to St. Mary Magdalene sometime in the 9th century AD. When Saunière carried out his renovations, he reinforced the Magdalene theme with a statue at the entrance to the church and episodes in the life of Mary Magdalene depicted inside the church. There are stained glass windows of Mary Magdalene as the penitent sinner anointing Jesus' feet with oil, and with her sister, Martha, in the house at Bethany. The front of the main altar has a painting of Mary Magdalene in her grotto. Abbé Saunière painted this himself and it is thought to contain some message with regard to the source of his wealth. Although it is unlikely, it has also been suggested that the statue on the Visigothic pillar may be that of Mary Magdalene and not the Virgin Mary, as had previously been supposed.

Mary Magdalene has a fully established cult following throughout most of the Christian world, particularly in France. An extraordinary number and variety of phenomena bear her name - towns, hospitals, colleges, campsites, a megalithic alignment, a geological era, a state of emotionality and/or drunkenness, even a type of cake. The majority of churches and cathedrals bearing the name Notre Dame in France refer to Mary Magdalene, not the Virgin Mary. Clearly the importance of this lady is not to be underestimated. So, let us take a look at her now.

There are very few references to Mary Magdalene by her full name in the books of the New Testament. The unspoken assumption is that she was synonymous with sexual licence, and that any mention of female misbehaviour means sexual misbehaviour and that it automatically refers to Mary Magdalene, who, for sixteen hundred years or so, has been charged as a prostitute. In reality, nowhere in the gospels does it say that she behaved with any sexual impropriety. They are unanimous in saying that she was at the foot of the Cross during the Crucifixion and that she was the first person to see Jesus after he had emerged from the tomb three days later. She apparently mistook him for the gardener. He told her not to touch him as he had not yet ascended to the Father, but to go and inform the other disciples that he was still alive. The only other reference to her by name is in Luke VIII where she is identified as having seven devils cast out of her, whatever that may mean. It has also been assumed by tradition that she was the Mary of Bethany who was the sister of Martha and Lazarus, whom Jesus raised from the dead. Once again, however, there is no actual naming of her fully in this regard. If the Church of Rome has proof that she was this Mary, they are keeping it to themselves.

To find out more about Mary Magdalene, we have to go to the Gnostic Gospels and here we find some very interesting and enlightening information. For a start, she had at least one Gospel all to herself - the Gospel of Mary. Found near the town of Nag Hammadi in Upper Egypt in 1945, in this and the other Gnostic Gospels - the Pistis Sophia, the Gospel of Philip, the Dialogue of the Saviour, Great Questions of Mary and many others, she is variously described as 'The Saviour's companion, the most important of the three women who were always with the Lord'. She is the Leader of the Apostles, no less, a position not even hinted at in the New Testament. The Church has always used Jesus' supposed lack of choice of women for his disciples as the reason why women should not be ordained. She is 'the Happy One, Beautiful in her speaking, the Spiritual Mariham, Inheritor of the Light'. Perhaps her most important title was the woman 'who knew the All'. This is far from the common prostitute and penitent sinner that the Church of Rome has tried to turn her into.

Her conflicts with Peter in the Gnostic Gospels reveal the antagonism felt by the male-oriented church towards the female; but it seems that, although it could suppress references to the importance of Mary Magdalene in the life of Jesus, it could not actually deny or falsify them except by default, omission and inference.

Most controversial of all are the statements in the Gnostic Gospels indicating very clearly that Jesus had a very sympathetic physical relationship with Mary Magdalene and probably a sexual one as well. Since Jesus is said to have come from Heaven to live, suffer and die as a man, it is hard to understand why there should be such outrage at the thought that he might have done exactly what all men do sexually, and why Mary Magdalene has been cast as little better than the Whore of Babylon, when she probably had a perfectly respectable and loving relationship with the man, who, as well as being the Son of God, was born to be King of the Jews, as the genealogies in the New Testament go out of their way to point out. As King of the Jews, it would also be his bounden duty to father at least one son to continue the line.

Biblical Judaea was a very male-oriented society. Women were considered to be unclean for at least half their monthly cycle, like lepers, pigs, etc. They were certainly not allowed to preach in the synagogue and they were not allowed anywhere near the temple. The idea of Mary, a married woman, knowing the All and having the audacity to preach this to men would have been more than most orthodox Jews - Pharisees and Sadducees - could bear. Only a brazen woman, a harlot, would have had the gall to behave in such a way and so history, helped by the Church of Rome, has tarred her with that brush. However, after the Crucifixion, she is said to have gone to Gaul i.e. southern France, via Ephesus, landing at Marseilles, which is named after her, spending the last thirty years of her life as a hermit in a grotto high in the mountains at St. Baume, dressed only in her hair and living on herbs and water. Her body was said to have been found in a sarcophagus at the church of St. Maximin in the region of Aix in 1270.

In mythology she is coupled with the Egyptian Isis, who also knew the All. She also has much in common with Venus/ Aphrodite and Helen of Troy. The name Magdalene, particularly in the form, MADELEINE, hints at a combination of the two names, MAGDALA and HELEN. Helen of Troy had Venus as her divine mother and Leda as her earthly one. Magdala was in the land previously called Canaan, which had been a centre of the worship of Astarte, the Mesopotamian Aphrodite. Magdala was a very prosperous part of Galilee. Doves were bred there for religious uses. Since these were used by the thousand on a regular basis, the Magdalene family would have been very well-to-do. Doves as a symbol of peace – it was a dove sent out by Noah that found dry land after the Flood – were sacred to Aphrodite. As a woman knowing love in all its forms – spiritual, maternal, emotional and carnal – Mary would indeed know the All in a way that Peter could not. No wonder his sense of self-importance took such a knock. He had been brought up in the patriarchy of the Old Testament and here was Jesus supporting what amounted to a heathen goddess.

It has been hinted that Mary Magdalene, or more specifically her womb and the fruit thereof, were the inspiration for the legend of the Holy Grail.

SECRET SOCIETIES

There seems to be a tribal element in human nature that makes men want to belong to a small elite group where each one is as important as the next, where they all know something that no-one else knows, everyone knows their place and they can face the world together. The common bond can be anything at all. It can be blood ties, family ties, military tradition, religious beliefs, sporting clubs, train spotting or any of a myriad other factors. The Rennes mystery appears to be of interest to several genuine secret societies and at least one that is known to lack a certain credibility.

Of course, by its very nature, there are elements of a secret society that will be known only to its initiates, and even then there may be secrets, which are revealed only as you progress through the hierarchy. There are, presumably, societies that are so secret, that they are not known about at all, except to their members. Still, publicly-known elements of the main secret societies associated with Rennes-le-Château can be discussed here and it is up to you, dear reader, how far you wish to pursue them. Let us start with the one known to have a spurious pedigree.

1) THE PRIORY OF SION

In the literature surrounding the Rennes mystery in the past forty-odd years, the Priory of Sion purports to be guarding the Merovingian lineage and supporting their claim to the throne of France. It is said to have been founded at the turn of the twelfth and thirteenth centuries by a breakaway group of Templars, and to have been behind the scenes in such matters as the bid for the throne of France by the House of Lorraine in the sixteenth century, the Fronde rebellion of the seventeenth century and the anti-Republican movement of the nineteenth century. However, all the documents appearing to authenticate its existence were lodged in the Bibliothèque Nationale in Paris in the 1950s and 60s. Not one of them has been found to exist as an original before their lodgement. In fact, all the documents in the file known as the *DOSSIERS SECRETS* are fakes or copies of fakes drawn up by two gentlemen known as Pierre Plantard and Philippe de Chérisey, who has admitted this several times. The *Dossiers Secrets* are outlined further on in this book.

From Paul Smith's meticulous research and correspondence with Gérard de Sède, the Bibliothèque Nationale and Lloyd's Bank International, it is quite clear that the Priory as it is portrayed in **THE HOLY BLOOD & THE HOLY GRAIL** is a form of hoax in that none of the documents appearing to validate its existence are genuine. The authors were told this but they have chosen to suggest that, all in all, while the validity of the documents may be questionable, there is no reason to doubt the existence of the Priory with regard to their particular hypothesis.

However, this is not to say that there is no real Priory of Sion today. Clive Prince and Lynn Picknett are convinced that the enigmatic 'Giovanni', with whom they had dealings while researching the origins of the Turin Shroud, was a genuine member of an organisation by that name. Other members of the Rennes Group have had correspondence from or meetings with people, who imply that they have intimate knowledge of the Priory and its aims. The Priory of Sion was also mentioned in a very rare book called **MATHEMATICA MEMORIALE** by the seventeenth century alchemist, Johannes Valentine. Be that as it may, it does not confirm that any of these organisations are the direct continuation of the one claimed to have been set up in the twelfth century, nor does it confirm that it still exists today to safeguard the interests of the Merovingian descendants.

What is probable is that a Priory of Sion did exist during the Middle Ages, that one also existed during the lifetime of Johannes Andrea three hundred years ago and that one exists today. Although its exact nature has not yet come to the attention of the author of this book, its purpose would seem to be the setting up of a benevolent form of government with a unified political system, a single religion and presided over by a 'legitimate' monarch. How this would be enforced in this age of television and the internet, instant global communication and the precedence of the individual over the community has yet to be seen.

Whether its Grand Masters included such illustrious names as Leonardo da Vinci, Botticelli, Nicholas Flamel, Robert Fludd, Isaac Newton, Victor Hugo and Jean Cocteau, as is claimed, is not provable here. If Pierre Plantard was a Grand Master, as is also claimed, it would be out of keeping with the tradition that seems to have been handed down. The Priory of Sion was set up to protect the dynasty, not to be the means of propagating it. Grand Master King René of Anjou was not Merovingian by birth. It was his wife Isabella of Lorraine who connected his offspring to the Underground Stream.

For the purposes of this book, the most that can be said is that a Priory of Sion may have been formed by a breakaway group of Templars in the Middle Ages. It may have been politicking away behind the scenes, supporting rival claims to the French throne down the centuries. It may well exist today. But its legitimacy as portrayed in most of the books published about the Rennes mystery since 1962 cannot be backed up by authentic documents lodged in the Bibliothèque Nationale

2) FREEMASONRY

When King Solomon built his temple nearly 3,000 years ago, he engaged the help of Hiram Abiff, Master Mason and King of Tyre, who provided skilled workmen including stonemasons, carpenters, etc. from Gebal to do the work, which took, according to 2 Chronicles VII v. 1, twenty years to complete, or seven years according to 1 Kings VI vs.1 and 38. However, no matter how long it took, Hiram did not live to see its completion since, according to legend: '. .at noon when the Men had gone to refresh themselves, as was his usual Custom, he came to survey the Works, and when he entered into the Temple, there were three Ruffians, supposed to be Three Fellow Crafts, planted themselves at the Three Entrances of the Temple, and when he came out, one demanded the Master a Word of him, and he replied that he did not receive it in such a manner, but Time and Patience would bring him to it. He not satisfied with that Answer, gave him a Blow (with a Setting Maul), which made him reel, he went to the other Gate, where being accosted in the same manner and making the same Reply, he received a greater Blow (with a Setting Tool), and at his third Quietus (with a Setting Beadle).' Hiram's corpse was discovered 15 days later by 15 Loving Brothers, by the Order of King Solomon, buried in a Grave 6 foot East by 6 Foot West by 6 Foot Perpendicular, covered in green moss and turf, to which they said *Thanks be to God, our Master has got a Mossy House*: so they covered him properly, placing a sprig of *Cassia* at the Head of his Grave.

The raising of Hiram Abiff's death is the initiation of a Master Mason. The legend of Hiram Abiff's death first appeared, as above in **MASONRY DIRECTED** by Samuel Pritchard in 1730 and taken here from **MYSTICAL CHRONOLOGIES** Third Edition Revised 1994 by Paul Smith.

Whatever its ancient and obscure beginnings, the Freemasonry that is common today began in the Middle Ages as a trade union for builders. This was an age of building on a vast scale. Eighty great cathedrals and churches were built in France in less than a hundred years. This required skill on a vast scale. Craftsmen needed a system by which their levels of skill could be recognised before they went to work on a building. Literacy as we know it just did not exist among the common people. Knowledge and ideas were passed on either verbally or in the language of symbols. Every art and craft had a symbolic language and the rituals of Freemasonry are part of the symbolic language of the builders of those times.

While it was in the hands of men who actually built the buildings, it was known as Operative Freemasonry. After the Grand Lodge was formally constituted in London on 24th June 1717, and the membership began to change from skilled craftsmen to men who had no professional link with building, it changed its name to Speculative Freemasonry, meaning thinking freemasonry or builders of ideas rather than bricks and mortar. It spread across the English Channel into the heart of Europe and took on a different character. Because of the universal nature of its religious recognition, it acquired cult status and its ideas of tolerance and free-thinking attracted the most brilliant minds of the day. It was also an ideal vehicle for the dissidents of the day, for the supporters of Gaston d'Orleans and his wife, of Lorraine, against Louis XIV in the 1650s and 60s, and for the monarchists against the republicans in Saunière's day.

The black and white chequered floor in his church is classic Masonic symbolism and indicates a strong whiff of Freemasonry in the Saunière affair. The Freemasons are thought to be the direct descendants of the Templars and to have had access to whatever secrets they possessed. If this included the secret, thought to have been guarded at Rennes, it is highly likely that the Freemasons would exert some sort of influence over Saunière and his activities.

3) THE COMPAGNIE DE SAINT SACREMENT

The Compagnie de Saint Sacrement was formed in 1628 by Saint Vincent de Paul (founder of the Lazarist order of monks and known as 'the conscience of the kingdom'), the architect Jean Ollier and the Bishop of Alet (near Rennes-le-Château) Nicholas Pavillon, to support the claim to the throne of Louis XIII's brother, Gaston d'Orleans, whose wife was of the House of Lorraine. It carried on its subversive activities after Louis' queen, Anne of Austria, gave birth to a son in 1638, right through to the coronation of Louis XIV in 1643, despite the end of the Fronde rebellion, defying the orders of Cardinal Mazarin (who was suspected of being the real father of Louis XIV) and the king, who finally ordered its dissolution in 1660. It was known to have been active for at least another five years and is thought to have survived into the twentieth century. As it was centred at St. Sulpice, it may well have had a significant influence on the nineteenth century occultists, who also made that church their centre. Saunière's known monarchist sympathies could have drawn him in as a member of the Compagnie.

4) SAINT SULPICE

'Each stone was placed in the image of another temple relating to the history of many and can be likened to the Unfinished Symphony by Schubert' - Jean-Luc Chaumeil.

The seminary of Saint Sulpice is seen to permeate every aspect of the Rennes mystery. Sulpice (although not a saint himself) was a chaplain to the Merovingian court. The feast day of Saint Sulpice is 17th January. The building was designed by Jean Ollier. It was situated on the site of the twelfth century abbey of St. Germain des Prés, which was the burial place for the Merovingian kings. Begun in 1645 and finished in 1777, it was the focus of the Compagnie de Saint Sacrement and all the subversive activity emanating from there. The line of the Paris Meridian is marked on its floor in the form of a brass rod running transversely from the south-west corner of the south transept to the north-east corner of the north transept. Its design, decoration and all the occult, subversive and heretical activities which have centred around it have caused Saint Sulpice to be called the 'New Temple of Solomon'.

When Saunière renovated his church, he decorated it in imitation of Saint Sulpice, containing his version of some of the essential elements. These are also contained in a curious document emanating from the Dossiers Secrets, called *LE SERPENT ROUGE*.

Over the porch of his church he placed the inscription TERRIBILIS IST LOCUS ISTE (This is a dreadful place - Genesis XXVIII v. 17 where Jacob raises a stone for a pillar). In the entrance the holy water stoup is supported by a statue generally thought to be a devil called ASMODEUS, who was said to have been trapped by Solomon into building his temple. More about him later. In the Chapel of the Angels in Saint Sulpice there is a painting by Eugéne Delacroix called THE DEFEAT OF ASMODEUS and containing the biblical quotation: "Terribilis ist locus iste." The figure of Asmodeus in the painting is similar to the one in Saunière's church.

There are four baptismal fonts forming a square in the Chapel of the Angels, each with a statue by Boizot representing wisdom, strength, grace and innocence - disguised versions of the four elements, earth, air, fire and water, carved openly as such in the entrance to Saunière's church. The statue of Notre Dame on the Visigothic pillar in Saunière's garden is surely an echo of the Saint Sulpice Chapel of Notre Dame du Pilier. Perhaps the altar painting of Mary Magdalene in her grotto represents Notre Dame Sous-terre, the Black Virgin, which is situated in the crypt of St Sulpice. The Stations of the Cross are reversed in both churches, but this is not unusual or extraordinary.

LES DOSSIERS SECRETS
(THE SECRET DOSSIERS)

Over the course of the 1950s and 60s various items relating to the story of Abbé Saunière and his treasure were deposited in a file in the National Library in Paris. From this file, which is known as *Les Dossiers Secrets* or the Secret Dossiers, or again the Priory documents, we learn all kinds of interesting things that have never appeared in the orthodox histories of the period. We are told, for example:-

- Of Abbé Saunière's discovery of parchments, jewels and gold coins during the renovation of his church and his subsequent visit to Paris after a 'incognito' visit by a member of the Hapsburg family. The Hapsburgs were the ruling family of the Austro-Hungarian Empire, the most powerful ruling family in Europe who were destined to fall a few years later as a result of the Great War.

- Of a marriage of the granddaughter of the Merovingian king Dagobert II to the grandson of the Visigothic king Wamba, from whom are descended the counts of Rhedae.

- Of the sale of the parchments to an Antiquarian Bookshop League in London.

- Of the fate of two tombstones originally commemorating the grave of Marie de Nègre d'Ables, the Lady d'Hautpoul of Rennes. One of these tombstones was engraved with the motto ET IN ARCADIA EGO and was originally removed from a tomb which was situated on the nearby Paris 0° Meridian and which was said to be illustrated in Nicolas Poussin's famous painting *LES BERGERS D'ARCADIE*. The other contained an inscription which, in a work of extraordinary ingenuity and complexity, turned out to be an anagram of the message decoded from one of the parchments.

- Of the Blanchefort family secret passed down through ages, hidden in the church at Rennes-le-Château during the time of the Revolution and passed on to the Fleury family at nearby Rennes-les-Bains.

- Of some of the history relating to Rennes-les-Bains, in

67

particular the occupation of the Romans, the stay of Blanche of Castille (not the mother of St. Louis but the wife of Pierre le Cruel) and some interesting information about the hot springs in the area. These features are born out to a certain extent by other documentation.

There are a large number of extraordinarily detailed genealogies including those of the Counts of the Razés from Visigothic times, of Godfrey de Bouillon, of the Counts of Saint-Clair, of the Lusignan family, of the House of Broyes (the Joinvilles), the Counts of Bar, of Gisors, Guitry, Mareuil and the Plantard family. Indeed members of the Plantard family along with some from the Chérisey family appear in several of these genealogies.

Most intriguing and most controversial is the list of Grand Masters of an hitherto unknown secret society, the Priory of Sion, which apparently came into being after a split between factions of the Knights Templar. More about both of these can be read elsewhere in this book.

Finally among the bits and pieces, we have illustrations of gravestones and other monuments attributed to one Ernst Stüblein, some maps, an extract from the journal of another secret society, the Hiéron du Val d'Or and a highly cryptic work called *LE SERPENT ROUGE*, which seems to be related to the Church of Saint Sulpice in Paris.

In the 1980s Pierre Plantard admitted to fabricating these documents along with the parchments, which were fabricated by his friend, Philippe de Chérisey. This fact was pounced on by the BBC Timewatch team in their documentary in1996, as evidence that the whole mystery is therefore a hoax. However, it should be pointed out that

a) Plantard and de Chérisey said that their parchment fabrications were based on originals and

b) that the fact that the documents may not be genuine originals does not mean that the information contained therein is false.

Genealogies, like the telling of history, are compiled by the victor to reinforce their position. He, or she, who pays the piper, calls the tune. Winner takes all, and if they were being paid so to do, the bards of old would exaggerate their patrons' claims to those winnings, i.e. thrones and kingdoms. The colleges of heralds exist to promote the claims of the great families of the realm. Who knows what offspring has been judiciously excluded, or indeed included in these rolls. After all, birth certificates and the parish register are relatively recent innovations.

PIERRE PLANTARD ST. CLAIR

"The best poker player I have ever met." – Henry Lincoln to a meeting of the Saunière Society in 1993

It has been suggested that the incumbent heir to the Merovingian throne is a gentleman by the name of Pierre Plantard St. Clair. The two names, PLANTARD and ST. CLAIR, appear in the Priory of Sion documents, suggesting that these families took up the torch of dynastic succession after the failure of the House of Guise and Lorraine to secure the throne and the succession in the middle of the sixteenth century. However, there does not seem to be any independent evidence elsewhere to corroborate the Plantard claim. Apparently he has said it exists elsewhere in a secret location.

So, what do we know of Pierre Plantard St. Clair? With interests in archaeology, psychology and mysticism, he was a draughtsman in the 1950s, an ex-hero of the Resistance firmly entrenched in right-wing organisations with a strong attraction towards the ideals of service, chivalry and leading the youth of France in what he considered to be the right direction. At the beginning of the 1960s he was writing a book about the Templars when he read about Rennes–le-Château in a book on mysteries by Robert Charroux. He decided to change the subject of his own book to that of Rennes-le-Château and enlisted the help of Gérard de Sède, who had also just written a book on the Templars. He also enlisted the help of his friend, Philippe de Chérisey, who fabricated the documents appearing to authenticate the existence of the Priory of Sion, and hoped, no doubt, a best-seller would be born.

It cannot be said that there was a deliberate attempt to mislead or defraud the readership. It may have been more of a masquerade that got out of hand. It may have been a method, dear to secret societies and the like, of conveying information without revealing more of the source than is strictly necessary. If Pierre Plantard St. Clair and his family are genuine heirs to the throne, no doubt all will be made clear in the fullness of time. Meanwhile, in the early 1990s he decided to secure a permanent link with the Rennes area, by securing a plot for his tomb at Rennes-les-Bains. Unfortunately this plot was washed away in the floods that swept through the village in 1994. Pierre Plantard died in 2000 and was buried in Paris. It was reported at the time that his son might be picking up his torch. However, the latest news is that he has forgone that honour.

ARCADIA

ET IN ARCADIA EGO is the motto that has been linked with the Rennes mystery primarily through the painting by Nicholas Poussin. It is also said to have been the motto of the Plantard family since 1210. Arcadia has been the inspiration of poets, painters and playwrights since the Renaissance. It is usually seen as the image of an idyllic rural life where shepherds and shepherdesses wander happily with their flocks of sheep, playing their pan pipes with little or no thought for tomorrow, no taxes to pay, no mortgage, no deadlines.

However, life in the real Arcadia was somewhat different. It could be brutal, savage and cannibalistic. It probably hosted the annual Dionysian rite of tearing the king to pieces. Under matriarchal rule, the queen took a man as her consort once a year. For the whole of that year he would be given everything he could possibly want including of course the favours of the queen. At the end of the year, either in spring or in autumn, he would be sacrificed in a fertility rite to ensure the success of the next season's harvest. One of the most notorious rituals took place on Naxos, where the vine king was torn to pieces by the maenads in a drunken frenzy.

Arcadia was also known as the kingdom of the Bear, after its sacred animal. Perhaps the rite of sacrifice in Arcadia included some activity on the part of a bear. Maybe this ritual was changed by the Celts, whose passion for bear hunting preceded their passion for hunting the wild boar.

Arcadia was one of Greece's most ancient kingdoms and the descendants of its royal household are said to have formed links with the ancestress of the Merovingian kings. It was also the first of the Greek kingdoms to become a democratic state. Perhaps the mystery of Rennes-le-Château is linked to the fate of the Arcadian kings in exile?

Arcadia was also the home of a secret dualist church linked with the emergence of the Paterini, a highly influential Cathar group from Calabria in southern Italy.

THE UNDERGROUND STREAM

Heads of society and of state usually acquire their position by election, by force or by birth. In some quarters there is a tradition that the position of monarch is a sacred trust granted to families of a certain lineage for the purposes of saving humanity from various destructive factors, most notably from itself. From one of these families will emerge the Grand Monarch, whose lineage can be traced back to Adam in the Bible and who will emerge to save the elected few at the End of the World. This is one of the themes of the seer, Nostradamus, who lived in nearby Alet. Because this lineage originates from one source but branches out into many as the result of marriages and descendants, in the same manner as a river begins at one source but branches out into many tributaries and streams before reaching the sea, this eternal genealogy of the Grand Monarch is known as the underground stream. Various paintings are thought to allude to this phenomenon. The river Alpheus in Arcadia has been used to symbolise this branching of the royal families of Europe, most notably in a picture possessed by King René of Anjou. The Merovingians seem to have been a major tributary of this underground stream and there now seems to be strong evidence that, by virtue of his ancestry, which goes right back to at least the last years of the Merovingian dynasty, Godfrey de Bouillon was probably in direct line, with his heirs, to carry on this dynasty by right.

ET IN ARCADIA EGO

In the coded parchments, SHEPHERDESS is usually accepted as referring to a painting called *LES BERGERS D'ARCADIE* (the Shepherds of Arcadia) by the French painter, Nicholas Poussin. He painted two versions of this picture and the one which is thought to refer to the Rennes mystery shows a shepherdess and three shepherds standing round a tomb against a landscape in which certain features of the Aude valley seem to be recognisable. One of the shepherds is kneeling in front of the tomb pointing at an inscription which can barely be seen as ET IN ARCADIA EGO. This theme is thought to have been based on a poem called ARCADIA by the Italian poet, Jacopo Sannazaro. A tomb which was thought to be that in the painting was discovered a few miles away at the little settlement of Les Pontils, but the owners destroyed it after being inundated with Rennes hunters. However, there is no record of a tomb being there in Poussin's time and there is an ongoing debate as to whether the background landscape of the picture is the same as that which is behind the tomb. This tomb was known as 'the tomb of Arques', Arques being a village with a very distinctive château a mile or so down the road from Les Pontils. Until recently Poussin was not known to have had any connection with this area. He is now known to have spent 3 years in Lyon before going to Rome. From Lyon, he could easily have spent time in the Aude Valley and got to know its landscape, which he reproduced in his paintings. As an artist, he would easily commit visual details to memory for use in later paintings – as he did with the Château Gaillard near his birthplace in Normandy.

The shepherd's scene also appears in a bas-relief on a stone monument called THE SHEPHERDS MONUMENT at Shugborough Hall in Staffordshire. Shugborough Hall is the seat of the Earls of Lichfield, a family steeped in Freemasonry. There is also an inscription on the monument which has recently been deciphered.

Another setting for this scene is the monument raised in Poussin's honour by the French politician and writer, the Viscount Châteaubriand, in Rome.

NICHOLAS POUSSIN

Nicholas Poussin, who is known as the father of French classical painting, was an artist of extraordinary complexity and he is known to have incorporated many layers of meaning into his pictures. The majority of these have mythological themes. According to Professor Christopher Cornford of the Royal College of Art, *LES BERGERS D'ARCADIE* is constructed along geometric lines with the pentagon as the central figure but using archaic rather than modern i.e. 17th century principles. Other paintings of his which are thought to be connected with the Rennes mystery are *LA PESTE D'AZOTH*, which shows the Philistines dying *en masse* after capturing the Ark of the Covenant from the Hebrews, *WINTER*, which shows the biblical Flood with a serpent in the foreground and Noah's Ark in the distance and *TIME DISCOVERS TRUTH*, another mythological theme.

Poussin was also mentioned in an enigmatic letter from abbé Louis Fouquet, later to become archbishop of Narbonne, to his brother, Nicholas Fouquet, Superintendent of Finances to King Louis XIV and the richest and most powerful man in France. This letter refers to a secret, known to Poussin, that will confer great fortune that kings will not get out of him and will not be known for centuries to come. Poussin's motto was *'Tenet Confidentiam'* - 'He keeps in confidence.'

A great deal of secret knowledge was circulating at this time under various guises such as the Arcadian Academies and the Rosicrucian Society. Men such as Galileo, Francis Bacon, Tycho Brahe and Isaac Newton, were studying the universe, its origins and its compositions under the title of Natural Philosophy, discovering (or maybe rediscovering) such facts as that the Earth went round the Sun and that Jupiter had satellite moons. Although its power was waning, this still meant death at the stake for heresy if the Church of Rome took an interest, so information was passed around in various coded and symbolic forms. It is quite possible that Poussin had encoded such information in his pictures, if you know what to look for, and that this is what is meant in the letter. After all, without the key, neither kings nor popes would be able to discover the information, wherever it was hidden – and great benefits would accrue from knowing such information – most notably the stranglehold of the Vatican would disappear.

NICOLAS FOUQUET

In 1661 Louis XIV had Nicolas Fouquet arrested for misappropriation of funds and for sedition. All his goods and property were promptly confiscated, a situation reminiscent of Philippe le Bel and the Templars. However, he ordered that none of his papers should be touched. He went through those personally in private. Fouquet's trial lasted for four years and at the end, uncharacteristically for him, the king demanded the death penalty. The court, however, backed by the Compagnie de Saint Sacrement, insisted on banishment. In 1665 Fouquet was imprisoned for life and, on the king's instructions, kept completely isolated. He was forbidden any form of communication, including writing materials, and any soldier who may have conversed with him was hanged or sent to the galleys. He is thought to have been the model for Alexander Dumas' **THE MAN IN THE IRON MASK**. After Poussin's death, Louis got hold of *LES BERGERS D'ARCADIE*, which he kept in his private apartments and allowed very few people to see it.

THE FOUQUET LETTER

This is the text of a letter to Nicholas Fouquet from his younger brother, who had been entrusted with a secret mission to Rome in 1656.

'I have given to M. Poussin the letter that you were kind enough to write to him; he displayed overwhelming joy on receiving it. You wouldn't believe, sir, the trouble that he takes to be of service to you, or the affection with which he goes about this, or the talent and integrity that he displays at all times.

He and I have planned certain things of which in a little while I shall be able to inform you fully; things which will give you through M. Poussin, advantages which kings would have great difficulty in obtaining from him and which, according to what he says, no-one in the world will ever retrieve in the centuries to come; and, furthermore, it would be achieved without much expense and could even be to our advantage, and they are matters so difficult to inquire into that nothing on earth at the present time could bring a greater fortune nor perhaps ever its equal.'

BLANCHEFORT & THE LORDS OF RENNES

In 1156 Bernand de Blanchefort is thought to have concealed something near Rennes-le-Château in a hiding place excavated by German miners. He conferred land around Rennes-le-Château and Le Bézu to the Templars. However, long before the Templars came to Albedune (Le Bézu), Pierre St. Jean, Lord of Rhedae, was made a Templar on 21st March 1147. A very important person, he was the Commander of Douzens and Brucafel, Preceptor (teacher) and Master of the Honours of Carcassonne and Rhedae.

Blanchefort was given to Pierre de Voisins in 1215. In 1285 there was a major preceptory at nearby Campagne-sur-Aude and Pierre reinforced the Templar presence, inviting a special contingent from Aragonese Roussillon to Le Bézu. As in Jerusalem, this contingent was supposed to be there to protect the pilgrims, this time on the road to Santiago de Compostela. But, as had been the case with the Holy Land, in reality the number involved would have been insufficient for that purpose. When the mass arrest of the Templars in France took place on 13th October 1307, this contingent was untouched by

Philippe. Its commander was Seigneur de Goth - the archbishop of Bordeaux, Philippe's pawn, was Bertrand de Goth. The mother of the Pope, Clement V, was Ida de Blanchefort. The implication of these relationships is that these families were all involved in protecting the secret.

When the Order of the Temple was destroyed, it is possible that many Templars sought asylum from the Lords of Rennes, giving them their valuables for safe keeping, mainly to prevent them from falling into the hands of the Hospitallers. The Voisins hid them in the church. However, in 1341 Jaques de Voisin was caught and charged with minting false coinage. Presumably he had been melting down the treasure he was supposed to be looking after. This is what Saunière may have found in the tomb he discovered on 21st September 1892,

THE D'HAUTPOULS

The d'Hautpouls were a family of considerable note who had given unstinting support to the monarchy for centuries. They became Lords of Rennes and Blanchefort in 1422. In 1644 a will which was said to be of great importance to the d'Hautpoul family disappeared. There has been a lot of speculation that its contents may have provided a clue to the secret kept by the Lords of Rennes and that this is why it disappeared. René Descadeillas, curator of the Municipal Library of Carcassonne and one of the most respected French writers on the Rennes mystery, having been investigating it on behalf of the Society for the Scientific Study of the Aude since 1957, thinks it established proof of Elizabeth d'Hautpoul's claim to the Blanchefort title. Her sister, Marie, wanted it for her son so that he could join the Order of Malta. Her cousin, Pierre François, wanted it for himself, to become head of the d'Hautpoul family and secure a position in the Languedoc 'Etat.' Elizabeth had probably hidden the will to keep it safe, and the secret of its hiding place died with her.

The Blanchefort title did not pass from François to his eldest daughter, Marie, who had married her cousin, d'Hautpoul-Félines, but to the youngest daughter, Gabrielle, who had married Paul-François-Vincent de Fleury. Despite fevered speculation, there is no mystery about this. The rule of aristocratic inheritance is 'No land, no title'. The Blanchefort lands and ruins were part of Gabrielle's dowry, so her husband took the title quite legitimately.

In 1834 the Marquis Amand d'Hautpoul-Félines became tutor to the young King Henry V, Count of Chambord and later husband of Marie-Thérèse Archduchess of Austria-d'Este, who donated three thousand francs so generously to Saunière's fund in 1886. The Marquis refused to take any payment for the privilege. He had shown his support for the Duke of Bordeaux several times and was held in high esteem. In fact it was the d'Hautpoul's unstinting loyalty to the monarchy which is thought to have been why the Archduchess was so generous to Saunière.

In 1848 General d'Hautpoul had an army of twenty-five thousand troops ready to support the Duke of Bordeaux in his attempt to regain the throne from the Republicans. But neither Henry nor his princes were made of the same stuff as his ancestors and the attempt fizzled out, many of them fleeing to England in the process. With no Bourbon to support, he joined forces with Prince Louis Napoleon in his candidature for the Presidential Election on 10th December 1848.

MARIE DE NÈGRE D'ABLES

Marie de Nègre d'Ables was the only daughter of François de Nègre and Toinette Gaichier Roquefeuille. Born in 1713, she was the granddaughter of Thimoleon, Seigneur d'Ables et Niort, who shared the Lordship of Niort with the d'Hautpouls, the family she married into, becoming the Marquise d'Hautpoul and a very important lady.

Like the British name 'Black', the name 'de Nègre' is not unusual and it may have originated from one of the many families involved in the exploitation of 'black labour' from Africa during the sixteenth to nineteenth centuries. On the other hand, this particular de Nègre family was established in the Sault country from the beginning of the fourteenth century. Since another possible origin of the name may refer to the noble families who participated in the reconquest of Spain from the Moors, it is more likely that this earlier event gave Marie's family its name. It is also worth pointing out that the name on all baptismal marriage and death certificates is Nègre, not Negri, as appears in so many books on the subject. Whatever its origins, Marie herself never used it in her signature, using only the surname, d'Ables. It has been suggested that she may have had a revulsion of what the name implied - the 'black trade' - and the pillaging of riches belonging to the American Indians, as well as feelings of pity. However, since her family may have had nothing to do with this element of society, she may have rejected it, since it was her guardian, François de Nègre, who was banished for the murder of the abbé Monge, the priest of Niort.

It was one of her tombstones that yielded the words MORT and ÉPEE, that decoded one of the parchments. It was her other tombstone, bearing the sign of an octopus, that Saunière is supposed to have defaced. It may seem curious that she should have been buried outside in the cemetery instead of in the tomb inside the church with all the other Lords and Ladies - if she was actually buried under those gravestones. However, it was apparently the custom that only men were buried inside a church. Women were buried outside. No doubt this was another of those indications of the subservient position of women in the eyes of the Church.

Saunière's father was a steward of the Marquis of Cazemajou, managing the flour-milling operation on the estate. This was a comfortable, responsible and influential position. The Cazemajous were cousins of the Nègre d'Ables and also co-lords of Niort. The Saunières of Montazels were renowned for their Catholic faith and their devotion to the monarchy, as was this part of France in general.

ABBÉ BÉRENGER SAUNIÈRE

Tall, dark and handsome, charismatic and with the physique of a rugby player, abbé François-Bérenger Saunière must have set more than a few hearts aflutter on his arrival in the little village of Rennes-le-Château in June 1885. Lively, intelligent, active and a born leader, he knew where he was going and how to persuade people to follow him. Just as he persuaded his childhood friends to follow him along the stream of Colours in search of the treasure that all the legends told of, so now he would persuade the women of his parish to seek treasure in heaven by spreading the word of the gospel and gaining converts. This he had learned he should do during his first ecclesiastical appointment as vicar of Alet, from the great Nicolas Pavillon, the radical seventeenth century bishop of Alet and co-founder of the Compagnie de Saint Sacrement along with Jean Ollier and Saint Vincent de Paul.

In fact, his appointment at Alet should have been the stepping stone to a much more illustrious career. Alet is a cathedral town, and while there he was plunged into a lively world of arts and politics which introduced him to a wide circle of very influential friends. So the question must be asked, why was his next appointment three years later to Le Clat, a tiny mountain village of some two-hundred-and-eighty-two inhabitants whose lives are devoted to the raising of sheep, only accessible by mule track, and his final appointment three years later to a similar situation at Rennes-le-Château? One possible answer may lie in the fact that a former priest of Rennes-le-Château, Antoine Bigou, had also been a priest at Le Clat. It was Antoine Bigou who is supposed to have left the message of the great secret of the d'Hautpoul family engraved on the gravestones of Marie de Nègre d'Ables before fleeing to Spain from the Revolution in 1789. Maybe in Carcassonne or in Alet he had learned something about abbé Bigou and the treasure of Rennes-le-Château that necessitated a stay in Le Clat. Maybe abbé Bigou had left something in Le Clat for the seeker that followed him.

Bérenger Saunière was a royalist and during the elections of 1885 he was a militant supporter of the Royalist cause – so much so that in December 1885, two months after the Republicans had won the elections, he was suspended from office, along with three other priests, by the Prefect of the

Aude for his reactionary speeches in the pulpit. Loss of office meant loss of salary, which was paid by the state, so his bishop, Monsignor Billard of Carcassonne, lent him two hundred francs and found him a position in the seminary at Narbonne. Finally in July 1886 the Prefect rescinded his sentence and he took up his appointment again at Rennes-le-Château, where he remained for the rest of his days.

His days in Narbonne were not unprofitable. He returned with a donation of three thousand francs from the Countess of Chambord. Saunière's annual salary was four-hundred-and-fifty francs, so this donation represented a sizeable sum. The Countess was the widow of the Count of Chambord, the recently deceased (1883) claimant to the throne of France. She also had no love for France, never setting foot there unless she had to – she was an Austrian princess, Marie-Thérèse of Austria-Este and had married Henri, Count of Chambord for reasons of state. She died in 1886, so it is quite possible that this donation came through the intervention of a third party. In fact another very illustrious Austrian is known to have visited Saunière on more than one occasion.

Known in the area as 'the stranger' or 'Monsieur Guillaume', this was the archduke Johan Salvator, the son of Leopold II of Austria, who in 1889 renounced his position from the Hapsburg family after a failed attempt to gain the throne of Bulgaria. In one of the Priory documents, *LE CERCLE D'ULYSSE* by Jean Delaude, it is suggested that a 'Monsieur de Chambord' (possibly the same as 'Monsieur Guillaume') visited Rennes-le-Château five or six times between 1885 and 1891, putting a total sum of over twenty thousand francs at Saunière's disposal. Moreover, this sum would not have been given to Saunière for nothing. It is thought that he was given instructions to look for something that would be of great value to this great family, and that he may have found it. The Count of Chambord had died without leaving an heir. The suggestion in *LE CERCLE D'ULYSSE* is that the documents found by Saunière in his church were genealogies and wills that would confirm rights of succession.

When Saunière was called to account for his income and

expenditure by bishop Beauséjour in 1910 he was uncharacteristically vague about amounts and sources. He kept meticulous accounts of his fees for saying masses, which for the most part were one or two francs. Yet when he was asked to produce his accounts for his buildings on his estate and their fittings and furnishings, all he could, or would, produce was a series of totals on a single sheet of paper, amounting to a hundred-and-ninety-three-thousand francs in all, saying that he had received some large donations, the donors of which wished to remain secret. This was quite within their entitlement and Saunière's rights; and despite the bishop's insistence that he reveal their source, to satisfy himself that nothing illegal such as trafficking in masses had not been taking place, this was the stance that Saunière maintained for the rest of his life.

It was common gossip that Saunière had discovered a treasure and he himself did nothing to discourage the rumour. It may have been true or he may have encouraged it to put people off the track of the real source of his income. In fact Saunière was not rich for the rest of his life. His court case against bishop Beauséjour, which went to the Vatican, was handled by a very wily canon by the name of Huguet. Dr. Huguet did not charge fees for his work, only expenses. But his expenses were prodigious. They involved spending a great deal of time in Rome, where he had many friends. At one point Saunière has to borrow money from a bank in Paris and he also makes plans to sell off some land to meet his needs. He certainly did not make money for himself. The sumptuous lifestyle he led was for the benefit of his prospective patrons. Naturally if you want rich people to give you money, you put on a show that befits their expectations.

Abbé Saunière was a born entrepreneur. He used every trick in the book to persuade visitors to his church to part with their money in order to improve its condition and to build up his estate into a place of pilgrimage. He had collecting boxes all over the place, he sold postcards, he ran a lottery, he collected stamps, he sold furniture, china, materials, wine and spirits, anything he could think of to make a franc. The family of his housekeeper lodged with him for twenty years and all their earnings were pooled to go into his fund.

This was an age of pilgrimages. Bernadette Soubirous of Lourdes had her visions in his childhood and by the time he arrived at Rennes-le-Château, Lourdes was thriving as centre of pilgrimage. A similar revival was happening at nearby Puivert where Notre Dame de Bon Secours was drawing in the pilgrims, having saved the villagers from a flood by inspiring them to break a rock above the village to let the waters out. Rennes-le-Château was virtually on the old pilgrimage route to Saint James of Compostela. If only Saunière could find an attraction to divert the pilgrims to Rennes-le-Château!

He needed a miracle – and indeed it could be said that by turning his dry, dusty, barren, hilltop estate into a cool, green oasis, full of exotic plants and animals, he worked that miracle himself. The church, which is dedicated to Mary Magdalene, is full of her images and symbols, and illustrations of incidents in her life mentioned in the bible. The buildings and the gardens were laid out in imitation of the road to Bethany, where Jesus forgave Mary Magdalene her sins. Thus, when their bodies had been healed by the waters of Rennes-les-Bains, the pilgrims came to Rennes-le-Château, which Saunière had turned into a place of place of spiritual healing.

As for any occult associations, to date there has not been a single shred of evidence to show that he had any esoteric knowledge whatsoever. That is not to say that he was completely ignorant of this side of things. Who knows what documents may be in the private hands of those not wanting to be publicly associated with the Rennes-le-Château affair? Marie Denarnaud was apparently seen burning sheaves of papers after his death. She said they were bank-notes, which is highly unlikely. She may have said that to deter people from finding out what was really written on them. His library was bought by a bookshop in Lyon, and this fact has opened up a whole new avenue of research into his activities.

Far from leading a secret life in Paris, or Spain, as some

have suggested, it now turns out that Saunière was leading a secret life in Lyon, where he had an address next to, and linked by hidden passage to, the secretary of a secret society known as the Martinists. He also had a horse and cart permanently available to him, the conditions for which did not require him to account for his journeys – a bit like having a car on a permanent retainer with an unlimited mileage agreement. It is thought he used this transport to take him high into the Pilat massif about sixty kilometres from Lyon., to a place where there is a chapel with an image of Mary Magdalene virtually identical to that in the church at Rennes-le-Château.

THE MISSION

What WAS Saunière's mission of 1891? Was he playing John the Baptist to an unknown 19th century Jesus? In 1885, in a sermon that resulted in him being given a year's suspension in Narbonne, he thundered from the pulpit 'The Republicans! This is the devil to be vanquished! These are who should kneel before the weight of religion and its adherents! The sign of the Cross is victorious and it is on our side!'

The church at Rennes-le-Château is full of monarchist symbolism. The river Jordan represents the line of David, the eternal genealogy of the Grand Monarch, one of the themes of the seer, Nostradamus. Christ represents the French kings, signifying that God is on their side. But are they literally descended from Him? In the Christian religion kings should be made in the likeness of priests. They become divine because they have been anointed by a priest. This was the problem the early Church had with the Merovingian monarchs, who were kings by right of birth. They did not need the sanction of the Church. They were above it. The only way the Church could exercise its influence was to encourage the extermination of their line and replace them with their anointed conquerors, the Carolingians, beginning with Charlemagne, and mould them into the tradition of the

Church. According to Edith Seton in **THE PIEBALD STANDARD**,(p. 276) in the late 15th century the style of the king's dress was that of a sub deacon at mass. The tunic was raised on the left shoulder as was the chasuble of a priest. The inscriptions, CHRISTUS VINCIT, CHRISTUS REGIT, CHRISTUS IMPERAVIT surrounding the Calvary installed by Saunière in the churchyard in 1897 are the opening words of the French coronation anthem. The figure of Jesus found in the church represents the French king.

PENITENCE! PENITFENCE! Did these words, also engraved on the Visigothic pillar, hint that the mission was a goal of the Blue Penitents of Narbonne? This was an austere order that modelled itself on the Brotherhood of Bethany - Lazarus, Martha and Mary Magdalene, whose imagery dominates not only the church but his estate too. The sermon at the rededication of his renovated church was given by a Lazarist monk.

Was he the guardian of the Hidden Pope? Recently come to light is a religious sect in Canada whose members are the guardians of the Mystical Pope, the spiritual counterpart of the Pope of the World in the Vatican. Interestingly, the third secret of Fatima is thought to include the message that there will be two popes.

LORRAINE - LA REINE – RENNES. The first Station of the Cross in Saunière's church depicts an old man, *UN AINE*, holding a golden egg, *UN OEUF DE L'OR*, standing behind Pontius Pilate, who is wearing a veil, *DEGUISE*. Modify the word order and we get *UN OEUF DE L'OR, AINE, DEGUISE*. Modify the meanings as we might hear them spoken and we get *UN NEUF DE LORRAINE ET DE GUISE* (A new one from Lorraine and de Guise). Of all the strangers who came to visit during Saunière's lifetime, one of the most eminent was the Austrian Archduke of Hapsburg-Lorraine, the family that currently holds the title of the House of Lorraine. Was Saunière preparing for the new claimant? Or was he himself eligible? The strange act of homage on his death was not customary at the passing of an ordinary parish priest. Was this the message he was going to proclaim from the hundred-and-fifty-foot tower he was planning to build?

The year 1891 saw the renaissance of the cult of the Virgin. The statue of the Virgin of Lourdes that Saunière installed next to the presbytery, and the photograph of him standing beside it looking up at her, demonstrate a devotion to her; and the words MISSION 1891 carved onto the visigothic pillar on which she stands probably refer to the pilgrimage of Notre Dame de Bon Secours at Puivert, which began that year, and whose success Saunière was hoping to emulate at Rennes-le-Château. Everything else on his estate, however, except for a picture of Saint Thérèse of Lisieux in the villa, is infused with images and symbols of Mary Magdalene. There is a photograph of him standing at the door of the church in all his finery. My own opinion is that Saunière had a great respect for the Virgin of Lourdes and that of Puivert, whose qualities as the Virgin Mary can be idolised but not emulated. However, his real devotion was to Mary Magdalene, the 'penitent sinner' with whom everyone can identify.

THE MAQUETTE

In 1992 a a maquette (the final drafting stage of a model), was introduced into the Rennes mystery as having been ordered by abbé Saunière in 1916 shortly before his death. Because the foundry in Aix was unaware of his decease, it was never completed. This artefact is highly controversial for several reasons, not the least being that there is no mention of it in any of his papers, which circumstance its current owner, André Douzet, says is due to the fact that it was part of his secret life in Lyon. While the maquette appears to depict a Crucifixion setting, the landscape is not Jerusalem; nor is it the Rennes area. As well as showing the tomb of Joseph of Arimathea, a most extraordinary feature is the Tomb of Christ. Most controversial of all, perhaps, André Douzet says that the message that Saunière had hidden on the model relates not to Rennes-le-Château, but to an area in the Corbieres, near Durban, known as Opoul-Perillos. He says that the former Lords of Perillos were guardians of a great secret and that, if death had not intervened, this is what Saunière would have conveyed by way of this model.

ABBÉ HENRI BOUDET

In France the man who is the focus of most attention is the one who probably would least want to attract attention. Abbé Henri Boudet was an erudite, scholarly enigmatic man who was the priest of Rennes-les-Bains for forty two years. Born on l0th November 1837 at Quillan into a well-to-do family connected with the iron-works near Axat, he studied for the priesthood at the seminary of Carcassonne, becoming a priest in his twenty-fifth year in 1862. After taking up appointments at Durban in the Corbières, at Caunes near Minerve and at Festes et Andres, Kercorb, he finally came to Rennes-les-Bains in 1872 where he remained until his retirement in 1914 after an enormous rent rise was imposed on the presbytery by the anti-clerical municipality.

He was held in great affection by his parishioners, who certainly considered him to be a cut above the rest. 'A superior man' was one phrase used. Perhaps his most important quality (or 'gift from God' as he would probably have seen it) was that he was a natural healer. He had a magnetism about him that convinced many people that he had healed them of their ailments. "The expression in his eyes was hard to bear," said one of his parishioners. "He knew secrets." He also knew all about the healing properties of plants. He was obviously the sort of man who caused spirits to brighten up when he entered a room; who brought a smile to people's faces on meeting them. Even the weather was said to improve when he was around. "What awful weather!" people would say. "If M. Boudet was here, it wouldn't last long." The thermal springs at Rennes-les-Bains have been used for medicinal purposes since pre-Roman times and Boudet realised that his mission in life was to see to the spiritual healing of the visitors to his parish.

He was a keen photographer and amateur archaeologist. He

presented several of his finds to the Archaeological Commission at Narbonne. He also found two statues of Venus; one of which he gave away as being too demonic for his taste and the other he insisted should remain buried. He took many photographs of the donjon at Arques, which seemed to hold a particular fascination for him.

Like Saunière, he was a great walker and spent a great deal of his time walking and studying the countryside around him. He had a lifetime's fascination for the great stones of the region and was particularly interested in the ancient megaliths, which abound in the area. In a note to a neighbour priest he said, "I enjoy the greenery on fine days but I like the winter when the greenery no longer hides the stones." His was the age when so much historical research was being carried out in the safety and comfort of academic libraries. Boudet was one of the pioneers of field research, actually going to the places whose history he was studying, rather than drawing conclusions by trawling the writings of other historians from the sanctuary of his study. It took him nine years to write the book, which is said to be crucial to unravelling the secrets of the area - **LA VRAIE LANGUE CELTIQUE ET LE CROMLECH DE RENNES-LES-BAINS** (The True Celtic Language and the Cromlech of Rennes-les-Bains). He published it finally at his own expense in 1886, a year after Saunière came to Rennes-le-Château. Sixteen years his elder, he became Saunière's friend and mentor and it is thought that he was the instigator behind Saunière's discoveries. It is known that Saunière received a lot of money from Boudet through Marie Denarnaud.

LA VRAIE LANGUE CELTIQUE ET LE CROMLECH DE RENNES-LES-BAINS

In essence, what Boudet argues on the surface in his book is that, although the Celts were known to have used Greek, their own language was English and their history and culture is preserved in the spoken English language. Thus, by giving place names an English pronunciation, many important things can be learned about their ancient history. It is important to stress that he does not say that the name should be translated into English, just that the Languedocian spelling should be pronounced as if it was an English word.

For example, rather than being defined in the conventional way as the land where the word for YES is OC, he pronounces Languedoc as LAND OAK meaning THE LAND OF THE OAK TREE. The oak tree was the most important tree in the Druid culture and alphabet. It was the tree under which all the most important decisions were made and around which cultural events took place. It was the Royal Tree. The importance of the oak to the Druids and the Celts cannot be over-emphasised. Boudet states that Rennes in Brittany and Rennes in the Aude valley were the most important centres of the Gaulish Celts. Both places fulfilled the same function. That is why they have the same name. In fact, using Boudet's pronunciation technique, Rennes in spoken English is WREN, the bird, and to the Druids the wren was the spirit of the oak tree and thus the most sacred of birds.

In his book he also suggests that, contrary to the received wisdom that the roots of the English language lie in ancient Greek, Hebrew and a host of other languages, the Celtic language in the form of spoken English is in fact the mother tongue and that all the languages that we consider seminal, are variations of Celtic English. Of course, this sounds as preposterous to most people today as it did in Boudet's time. But it should not be overlooked that not only was he a gentle, humorous man with a love of word games and a twinkle in his eye, he was also intelligent, highly educated and a considerable scholar of English. Bearing in mind the age-old animosity between our cultures, coupled with France's traditional pride in her intellectual and idealistic aspirations, the thesis underlying Boudet's proposition deserves some consideration.

There is, for example, a considerable similarity between the Celtic and Hebrew alphabets. Contrary to popular belief that they wrote nothing down, the Druids wrote extensively in ancient Greek. Since they preceded the Greeks, it is logical to assume that their language and heritage also preceded that of the Greeks; and that they took advantage of the rise in Greek culture, including their technological advances such as lettering, to maintain, and perhaps extend their influence. We assume that English has developed from the grunts of a race of savages painted in woad. But we could be wrong. English is far more than basic Anglo Saxon rendered 'civilised' by Greek and Latin, as we are taught to believe in our own country. Today it is the universal language of business and technology. In Boudet's time it was the language of Empire. Three hundred and more years ago it was the language of Shakespeare, Milton and John Donne. No-one knows for sure exactly how English was pronounced before our own historical times. We can only make surmises by putting some kind of Nordic, or perhaps local accent to the words we find written down, a process not helped by the fact that the spelling there is by far from consistent. It is the most flexible language in the world, able to absorb any concept from any culture and to convert it into a readily usable form of words. One message of **LA VRAIE LANGUE CELTIQUE** is *LISTEN TO WHAT YOU HEAR RATHER THAN BELIEVE WHAT YOU SEE.*

So, Boudet may have a valid point. Anyway, it can be fun and quite instructive to do as he suggests, and you may come to some surprising conclusions. A Dutchman, Jos Bertaulet, has recently found a tomb at Notre Dame de Marceille using Boudet's book and it is highly unlikely that this is the only thing it will lead to. In fact it is said that it hides the secret to the locations of several treasures hidden in the area. And it is the last ten pages which are said to hold the answer to the mystery of Rennes-le-Château.

When studying these matters, we should always be careful not to take people and their activities out of their times and context. Saunière may have been looking for treasure; Boudet may have delighted in word games. But they were both nineteenth century priests, firmly rooted in the monarchist tradition, seeing their positions becoming daily more insecure due to the actions of the post-revolutionary, anti-monarchist, anti-clerical republicans. They were both born and bred, and lived out their lives, in an area traditionally out of step with orthodox Roman Catholic teaching (steeped in heresy, the Church would have said) and with a history of persecution not seen elsewhere in Europe until the middle of the twentieth century. Maybe they had to live lies sometimes to keep alight in secret the flame of truth as they saw it. To look at the situation through the eyes of a twentieth century English Protestant, Agnostic, Atheist or from a purely secular viewpoint may result in missing the essence of their activities completely.

A priest's mission is to serve God. If he is a Roman Catholic, his primary allegiance is to the Church of Rome and he carries out his mission by ministering to the people, both clerical and lay. He may be a healer, a teacher or a provider of spiritual or physical comforts. Boudet's gift was for healing. Saunière's mission is unclear. Both felt the need to spread the Word in the way that suited their talents best.

Things are rarely as they seem in the Rennes mystery. We have one parish priest living the life of the lord of the manor and another who was an authority on the finer points of pagan religion long before they had been made popular by Robert Graves and Sir James Frazer. They lived at a time when belief in the occult was on a par with New Age thinking today, but at a time when people were still occasionally being burnt at the stake for witchcraft. The last such burning in France took place in the Sologne in 1885, the year when Saunière was installed at Rennes-le-Château.

If Saunière and Boudet were involved in occult, anti-Catholic interests, what better cover than to appear to be the most devout of believers. Saunière would also have had good reason to carry on with unrecorded activities. As he seems to have been determined to stay in Rennes-le-Château, perhaps this was why he was not afraid to show pro-monarchist sympathies. After all, he only jeopardised his career, not his life, and he was able to carry on with his search or his mission or whatever he was doing.

That Saunière and Boudet were good priests, there can be no

doubt. Whatever their complaints about his nightly deeds in the cemetery, Saunière's parishioners insisted that he remained their pastor, refusing to attend the services conducted by abbé Marty, whom Mgr. Beauséjour sent to replace Saunière on his suspension. Instead they all insisted on attending the services he conducted in his chapel in the presbytery. Those who remember him today still talk enthusiastically about his qualities as a priest.

Despite the ridicule he received for his theories regarding the place of Anglo-Saxon in the linguistic history of the Languedoc, Boudet was highly regarded in his field academically and his work in general was received as a serious contribution to the linguistic study of the region. He was a regular contributor to the Société des Etudes Scientifiques d'Aude right up to the end of the 19th century. He died on 30th March 1915 at Axat, where he was buried with a curious headstone. It is of a closed book and the inscription I X I O Ɛ.

MYSTERIOUS DEATHS

As befits mysteries of this kind, there are rumours - sometimes substantiated, sometimes not - of the mysterious deaths of people closely associated with the Rennes enigma. Certainly an unusual number of priests have been found dead in mysterious circumstances. Although he was terminally ill with intestinal cancer, it has been alleged that abbé Boudet died in agony a few hours after being visited by some mysterious strangers. It is also rumoured that Saunière was visited by the same strangers just before his fatal heart attack in 1917. They were not the only priests in the area to be rumoured to have died after such visitations.

In 1897 abbé Gélis, a recluse in his seventieth year, had become so fearful of strangers that he would only open the presbytery door to exchange food and laundry with his niece, who had to remain on the doorstep with the door closed while he did so. Yet, despite his suspicions, on the eve of All Saints Day 1897 he seems to have opened the door to someone, who then struck him down with fire tongs before killing him with an axe. There was no sign of a forced entry or of whom he had admitted. There were signs of his belongings being searched, but if anything was taken, it was not money. His body was laid out carefully with his hands across his chest and despite the amount of blood that poured out, the murderer left no trace except for two drops on the stairs leading to his room. Two other things were left by chance or design, who knows? A packet of cigarette papers called LE TSAR and a piece of paper with VIVA ANGELINA on it.

A hundred-and-sixty years earlier, the guardian of Marie de Nègre d'Ables, François de Nègre, was banished for murdering the abbé Bernard Monge, curé of Niort. During his banishment he lent François d'Hautpoul the money to buy the late abbé's presbytery. François d'Hautpoul married Marie de Nègre d'Ables.

Noël Corbu, who bought Saunière's estate from Marie Denarnaud, was killed in a dreadful car crash which happened for no apparent reason on 20th May 1968.

Less than a month later, abbé Boyer, the vicar-general of Carcassonne, who was a keen investigator into the Rennes enigma, was badly injured in an accident near the Devil's Bridge on the Carcassonne road, just missing the same fate as Noël Corbu.

According to Lionel Fanthorpe, abbé Mazières, the parish priest of Villesquelande and a former lawyer, told Gérard de Sède 'This Rennes affaire is very gripping, but I must warn you. . .it is also very dangerous.' So, you Men in Black or whatever, let me say at once that I value my own skin far more than wanting to poke my nose in where it is not wanted. I'm no hero, believe me. Just let me know gently in a civilised manner if I am treading on anyone's sensibilities and I shall be quite happy to back off and keep my distance.

JANUARY 17TH

This is a recurring date in the Rennes Mystery. It is:
- the feast day of St. Anthony, whose temptation was the

92

subject of a painting by David Teniers the Younger and was mentioned in the coded parchments
- the feast day of St. Sulpice
- the feast day of St. Roseline, an increasingly important element linked to the Meridian
- the day of Marie de Nègre d'Ables' death
- the day when Saunière was supposed to have been struck with his fatal illness.
- a date used as a sign of recognition in various Priory-inspired material such the Sennier letter. This is a letter supposedly sent to Abbé Saunière just before his death.

ST. JEAN (ST. JOHN)

St. John has become an increasingly recurring theme in the Rennes mystery. He is said to have been the author of the fourth Gospel of the New Testament, also called the Gnostic Gospel. He occurs in many paintings which, although on the surface are portraying standard Christian themes and episodes, are thought to be conveying unorthodox information and beliefs for those 'with eyes to see.' There is a mannerism known as the 'John gesture' whereby the right hand is seen with the forefinger pointing at something or raised upwards. In **THE TEMPLAR REVELATION** Lynn Picknett and Clive Prince say that John the Baptist was the genuine Christ, not Jesus and that this was the secret guarded so closely by the Knights Templar. In the context of the Rennes mystery St. John and John the Baptist seem to be interchangeable.

St. John is the Order of the Knights Hospitaller, also called the Knights of Malta, the Order that absorbed many of the Templars on their dispersal in 1307.

Pierre St. Jean was the Lord of Rennes and owner of Blanchefort when the Order of the Templars was broken up.

Jean is the name of the godson said to have assassinated Dagobert II at Stenay in 679AD.

ST. JEAN is mentioned in a note to Marie Denarnaud written after Saunière's death and, in the context of the note, could be a code word for the secret matter to which Saunière was privy.

ASMODEUS

Asmodeus was the demon of lust, who personified rage and filled men's hearts with anger and revenge. He was the son of an angel and a mortal woman. His function was to sow discord in marriage and to encourage adultery. When Master Magician King Solomon forced Asmodeus and other demons to build the temple at Jerusalem, Asmodeus managed to seize his ring of power and hurled it to the bottom of the sea, exiling Solomon and reigning in his stead. But Solomon miraculously recovered the ring and imprisoned Asmodeus and the other demons in a large jar. When Asmodeus shows himself to men, he rides a dragon with three heads - a ram, a bull and a man. The magician must summon him bare-headed as a mark of respect. He can make the magician invisible and can lead him to hidden treasure.

SACRED LANDSCAPE GEOMETRY

The lands of the Earth are covered with ancient monuments in the form of mounds, megaliths, churches, wells, groves, etc. all of which indicate a highly organised and intelligent culture and with customs, traditions and beliefs of which we know very little. However, a great deal of research has gone into the location of these features, particularly in the past thirty years or so, and it has been shown that they were not random placements, but were put where they were for precise mathematical reasons.

Now, before those of you who come out in a cold sweat at the very mention of the words MATHEMATICAL and NUMBERS go off to lie down in a darkened room, let me reassure you at once that this section contains no sums, calculations, theorems, equations, etc. All it does is briefly describe the general ideas behind what has been found so far. This is a concise guide for everybody to understand, so the only numbers mentioned are the number of Plato's basic geometric shapes and a twenty-eight day cycle. The only measurements mentioned are the pole and the English mile.

94

Those of you who are gluttons for mathematical punishment will find all the calculations you want in the works of David Wood and Ian Campbell, Henry Lincoln, Mark Pawson, Michael Gabriel and Richard Andrews & Paul Schellenberger.

In the great age of church building, not only was architecture designed along classic geometric lines according to the Pythagorean principles of harmony, but when lined up with other ancient landscape features, they were located on points of geometric significance. In other words, they could be part of a straight line, a triangle, a circle, a square, a pentagon or perhaps a point of intersection of a far more complicated figure. These medieval churches were built on the sites of much older buildings, very often containing sacred wells. This is why it is called SACRED LANDSCAPE GEOMETRY.

The word TEMPLE, like the word TEMPLATE, means pattern. In his book, **ANACALYPSIS**, Godfrey Higgins says that every ancient community had its temple (i.e. every ancient sacred site) laid out according to a universal blueprint. So, large or small, using trees, megaliths, hills, buildings or whatever, each site was laid out using the same mathematical designs, principles and proportions but on different scales according to the nature of the congregation. So, although a small church serves different needs from a great city cathedral, its purpose is the same and they are both oriented to the east with the form of a cross built into them. A stone circle on a hilltop in Wales would have served a different community from Stonehenge on Salisbury Plain, but it will still have a sunrise orientation and a water course running underneath.

The megaliths of prehistoric times are some of the world's most enigmatic remains, especially the dolmens - the capstone poised on top of three or more supporting stones (see diagram) and rocking stones, whose one enormous stone is placed so precisely on top of a number of supporting stones that it can be rocked with a light touch of the hand. These huge flat stones have been estimated as weighing as much as twenty five tons.

Dolmens and standing stones seem to be associated with currents of underground water and of electrical energy. The megaliths are found to emit an energy easily detectable by those who know how to experience it, dowsers in particular. The energy fluctuates according to the time of day and it waxes and wanes during a twenty-eight day cycle. It can be strong enough to provide an invisible barrier between the stone and the person approaching it, and it can be strong enough to throw a grown man off his feet.

The megaliths are all quartz based, and quartz, when compressed and struck, produces electricity. Our whole electronic and computer network is based on quartz technology. Quartz is composed of crystals of silica and the shapes of the crystals determine the nature of the quartz. Plato recognised the importance of shape when he defined the five fundamental shapes of solid matter - the sphere, the three-faced pyramid (tetrahedron), the six-sided cube, the eight-faced octagon and the twenty-sided polygon (dodecahedron). The shape, composition and orientation of the crystals in these megaliths are not like those found in quartz that occurs naturally. It may have been treated in some way before the stones were set and it could be this treatment that provides the connection between the stones and the power they emit. This power, which can be deflected with the use of amber, is thought to show up on photographs and cause anomalies in heat, light and sound wave bands.

The ancient people, so far as we can judge from the religion and traditions of people such as the native American Indians, who still have cultural links with their ancient past, revered the land as a whole, not just one spot, although some sites were more sacred than others. On a day-to-day level they lived not just close to the land, but in harmony with it. They knew where food could be found, where medicinal plants would grow and, most important of all, where to find water. We do not need water just to slake our thirst. We are water. Ninety-six per cent of our body is water. All living things are expressions of water sculpture. Every giant tree is the result of a tiny seed taking in water and stretching its components as far as they will go in mathematically determined directions.

On a highly sophisticated level, there was an element amongst them that acquired a knowledge of mathematics that only a comparatively small percentage of the population possess today. For an earthbound species, they spent a great deal of time and energy contemplating the cosmos and the mathematics of the Universe, particularly that of the night sky. The constellations of the Great Bear, Orion and the Lyre, and of Sirius, the Dog Star, held secrets of great importance for people all over the world, not just in the Middle East. Recently it has been surmised that the Earth has been subjected to several cosmic catastrophes in the remote past - comet or asteroid strikes, perhaps - and that these stars acted as pointers. It has even been suggested that thousands, maybe hundreds of thousands of years ago, the Earth had visitors, perhaps even settlers, from outer space coming in from the direction of these stars and that it was these visitors that gave rise to the legends of the Gods. There are also suggestions that homo sapiens was the result of genetic engineering by these visitors, most of whom left when one of these cosmic disasters was about to strike once more. The history of these visitors can be deduced from the legends of Sumer and Ancient Egypt.

There are several theories as to what may lie behind the layout of the sacred landscapes. One is that they contain a mapping system of the energy currents that can be tapped beneath the Earth's surface. Another is that they contain astronomical information regarding past and future strikes by bodies from Outer Space. It is knowledge of this nature that is said to have been possessed by the Hermetic and Secret Societies such as the Templars and the Cathars and to have been suppressed by the Catholic Church. It is said to have been imprinted on the landscape as a permanent record for those with the eyes to see and the intelligence to understand - and hopefully the ability to do something about it before it is too late.

In Wales many of the megaliths have the name ARTHUR -

in Welsh 'Arthur' means BEAR - and PIGWN or PEGWN, which means POLE as in a magnet. The long axis of the dolmens is usually north-south and even after four thousand years, some of them are still pointing upwards towards the constellation of the Great Bear, which continually circles the Pole Star.

The Rennes plateau, also known as the Haut Razés, abounds with megaliths among which abbé Boudet enjoyed so much of his time. Although many of the stones he classes as megaliths are actually natural outcrops of rock, most are part of the Cromlech of Rennes-les-Bains. The most significant of these is probably the dolmen called CAP DE L'HOMME on the hill above the church at Rennes-les-Bains .

PARCHMENT GEOMETRY AND THE TOMB OF GOD

In 1996 Richard Andrews and Paul Schellenberger arrived on the scene amidst an extraordinary publicity campaign of secrecy and tales of huge advances for their book. What they suggested was that a treasure of immense spiritual importance, the body of Jesus, no less, was buried somewhere under the slopes of Pech Cardou, near to the tomb at Les Pontils, and that all this could be deduced from the geometry and the coded messages hidden in the parchments. The geometrical patterns formed by certain characters in the actual layout of the parchments are as significant as the words themselves. The BBC Timewatch team ostensibly destroyed their credibility by pointing out that none of the documents on which they were relying had ever been seen by they themselves or anyone outside of the Priory team. However, this did not deter them from maintaining their position. Nor has it prevented a growing number of geometricians, slide rule and GPS (Global Positioning Satellite) receiving equipment in hand, angling to find what might be hidden in the area.

As a non-mathematician myself, the numbers and diagrams indicating the location of something likely to be very important are very persuasive to look at, and I am assured that anyone who checks them independently cannot fault their calculations. Whether the mountain really does contain the body of Jesus though remains in question. What could constitute incontrovertible proof?

More recently Patrick Byrne has also identified the same site as containing a treasure of immense spiritual importance but much older than Jesus. He suggests that the lost secret of the Freemasons relates to the Knights Templar having concealed the Ark of the Covenant in a temple constructed deep within the mountain.

Maybe more telling is the notion that the intelligence services of various nations – French, British and Israeli among others – are said to take a very close interest in anyone ferreting around in the area. The site had already been located in 1971 by a Belgian engineer, who said that its contents were protected by a series of lethal booby traps. So, you intrepid mystery hunters, if you feel drawn irresistibly to the slopes of Pech Cardou with shovel and pick, beware, take care and make sure your nearest and dearest know what time to expect you home for tea.

THE MERIDIAN

A recurring constant in the Rennes mystery is the Paris 0° meridian. There had been fierce competition between the British and the French to establish a zero meridian which the British eventually won when in 1884 an international conference in Washington USA agreed it should be set at Greenwich. This has not perturbed the French however. They still recognise the zero meridian set in Paris by the Cassini brothers in the mid-1680s. There is a brass rod marking its position in the church of Saint-Sulpice.

The meridian is set so that it runs through the greatest possible land area of France. This mirrors, by design or by chance, the Ancient Meridian that passed through the Great Pyramid in Egypt which travelled north to south through the world's greatest possible land mass. And for reasons unknown, François Mitterand, when he was president of France had the glass pyramid outside the Louvre installed on the Paris meridian.

The meridian passes down through Carcassonne and exactly through the rock on which the tomb at Les Pontils was situated. This is the tomb that was said to be the model used by Nicolas Poussin in his painting *LES BERGERS D'ARCADIE* and is also known as the tomb of Arques. Running down to the edge of the Pyrenees, it ends just past a tiny village called Py (pi - π - for the mathematicians among you to ponder).

The meridian's intrinsic relevance to the Rennes mystery is not known yet, but it features in all the geometry discovered so far. In fact it is not the only meridian to occur geometrically. There is a meridian known as the Rose Line which runs close to the Paris meridian and this is integral to all the new geometry being found implicating a site of great importance in the area of Pech Cardou.

A meridian is a marker not just of space but of time and it is possible that the meridian has an importance linked to time. The zero meridian implies the line where time begins. Possibly it locates something to do with the beginning of a very important period in history. No doubt all, or at least some, will be revealed in the fullness of time.

THE MYSTERY OF RENNES-LE-CHÂTEAU

The mystery of Rennes-le-Château is far bigger than Bérenger Saunière. His significance seems to be that he and his activities touch on so many other matters to which the area has played host.

The Lords of Rennes did guard a secret. They were very influential in the Templar movement. The Templars were thought to possess something that gave them great wealth and power. Guesses range from magic heads to the Ark of the Covenant.

King Dagobert II was said to be married to Gisela, the Visigothic princess of the Razés and mistress of Blanchefort and it is in this area that their son, Sigisbert, disappeared. However, this information comes from the Priory documents and there is no formal historical proof elsewhere of this marriage or its issue.

The Visigoths were fantastically wealthy thanks to their mastery of blue steel and wine making. In 410 AD after he had sacked Rome, Alaric did bring the treasure of the temple from there to southern Gaul, i.e. the Languedoc and legends of its burial abound in Toulouse, Carcassonne and Rhedae, among other places. They were buried with their wealth in secret locations.

Bernard de Blanchefort was renowned as an alchemist. One of the towers of his château is called the Alchemy Tower. Who knows what he might have discovered in the course of making his concoctions? Around the château, the land abounds with metallic deposits and there was a great deal of mining and metallurgical activity there.

Known as Rhedae during the thirteenth century, Rennes-le-Château was one of the main Cathar strongholds. Its inhabitants were massacred during the Albigensian crusade. Montségur, their last stand and the place from where their secret was supposed to have been born away the night before they were all cremated, is not so far away that a safe hiding place there could not have been reached in the middle of the turmoil.

Rennes-le-Château belonged to the de Charnys, who, as well as being the first family to have owned the relic known as the Turin Shroud, (although there is no evidence that they ever claimed it was the actual cloth that Jesus was wrapped in after the Crucifixion), were part of a group of families all protecting claims to occupy the throne of France. These claims are all related to the bloodlines of the biblical House of David and the Tribe of Benjamin.

There are innumerable pre-Christian, Roman, Greek, Egyptian, Celtic, Druid and pre-historic remains in the area. These were abbé Boudet's passion. He discovered the importance of the Rennes area to the Druids of southern Gaul and uncovered their history and culture in the language of the area. He also mapped out the megalithic monuments, which later researchers have to shown to be part of a vast figure of landscape geometry.

A temple of Isis in the area indicates long associations with the ancient Egyptians. Rennes-le-Château is one of the key points on a gigantic landscape pentagram, which could have been part of a huge Egyptian temple also laid out in the landscape. The mythology of the Egyptians coupled with the landscape features of the temple could suggest that Mankind was seeded by beings from another planet hundreds of thousands of years ago after which the Earth was hit by a cosmic disaster, probably in the form of a comet, and that it will suffer one again in the future. This can all be read in the mathematics of the temple.

New geometry leads us away from Rennes-le-Château itself over to the mountains to Pech Cardou. The gold and silver mines in this area were exhausted centuries ago, and the network of tunnels may conceal the body of Jesus, an explosive idea in religious terms, or indeed maybe something even more explosive physically. The Ark of the Covenant was a very dangerous piece of furniture with which to come into contact. Pech Cardou would provide an ideal repository.

France has a strong esoteric movement interested in the secrets of hermeticism, alchemy, astrology and all the hidden traditions of ancient European and Middle Eastern cultures. The nineteenth century Parisian occultists were seeking a powerful talisman known as the Talisman of Set, which was reputed to be hidden in the area. Set was also known as the Lord of Time. The Paris 0° Meridian, marker of space and time, runs through the area and there was a real contest between the French and English scientists of the day to set this meridian each in their own country. Flamsteed won the day and the universal 0° meridian of our planet was finally located at Greenwich. Meanwhile, the Paris 0° meridian is still marked by a cross on top of the Pantheon and a bar in the church at Saint Sulpice from where it runs through to the Rennes valley. During his tenure as President of the Republic, François Mitterand had the glass pyramid next to the Louvre deliberately installed in that position so that it is actually on the Paris Meridian.

Some people think Rennes-le-Château is the repository of an on-going politico-monarchical-religious struggle. Some think it is an arcane, mystical key to the secret of the End of the World. Some think it has a limitless treasure of gold and silver, although in all the digging that went on in the 1960s, 70s and 80s, nothing of any substance was found. For many people there is no mystery at all, merely a chain of interesting and not-so-interesting situations which can all be accounted for within the normal range of human experience. For them everything can be explained in terms of the facts that have already been made known, if researchers care to seek them out. They see many Rennes hunters as deliberately ignoring ordinary mundane facts and explanations in favour of the more fantastical.

The name of the Rennes valley is LA VALDIEU – The Valley of God. Set was the Egyptian God of Time who fell from grace. He has similar names and traditions in all the ancient cultures – Chronos, Saturn, Satan, Shaitan, Lucifer. These names are all inter-changeable with the meaning of time and also light. Several researchers think that the mystery of Rennes involves a cosmic event that happened to the Earth aeons ago and will happen again in the not-so-distant future. The mathematics needed to discover the existence of their message to us is so complex that it can only be deciphered when the mathematical skills of the culture have reached a certain level. The implication of this is that only when we have reached a certain plateau of intellectual ability will we be able to understand what is happening and take measures to lessen its impact. The thinking of researchers in this area is that the Church has known this all along and has prevented its knowledge from reaching the general populace for fear of losing control. The same could be said of all the initiates who are said to have kept this knowledge secret. Maybe they have all been afraid that if Mankind knows it can calculate when its end will come, people will be unwilling to spend their time doing hard graft for the ones who don't want to do it for themselves.

It is said that the final chapter of LA VRAIE LANGUE CELTIQUE contains the secret of the Rennes enigma. This chapter is about the Gauls changing their favourite hunting quarry from the bear to the wild boar. The word for BEAR in French is OURS. Pronunciation in English has two meanings:- 1) that which belongs to us and 2) a measure of time, HOURS. The French for WILD BOAR is SANGLIER. In spoken English this can be split into two words, SONG and LYRE. These were the trade marks of ORPHEUS, one of the most important figures of the ancient world and a founding figure of Dualism.

LIGHT

In an article emanating from the millennial secret society, L'HIERON DU VAL D'OR, it is said that to understand the connection between St. Denys, the patron saint of France, and Dionysos is to understand the secret of one of the great hermetic principles. The name ORPHEUS is composed of both the Hebrew and the Greek words for LIGHT; and the name of the constellation of the GREAT BEAR (our ancestors had their eyes constantly on the heavens) also means GREAT LIGHT. All these names have a close affinity with the word OR meaning GOLD.

Ultimately the mystery of Rennes-le-Château is the mystery of enlightenment. This means different things to different people. It can be historical, political, emotional, religious or spiritual. Those who find enlightenment at Rennes will find it according to the path they are following. For those who are looking for gold and silver or any physical manifestation, it may be worth considering the following. Orphism is another name for Dualism, the belief in the eternal conflict of the powers of Light and Darkness, the world of spirit being powered by Light, the physical world being powered by Darkness. When we look into our spiritual selves, we journey automatically towards the Light, as anyone who has had such an experience, be it the Light of understanding or even a near-death experience, will tell you. When we go out into the physical universe, into Space and to the stars, we go out into the dark towards bodies that will ultimately burn out.

WHAT OTHER AUTHORS HAVE TO SAY

ENGLISH AUTHORS

MICHAEL BAIGENT HENRY LINCOLN & RICHARD LEIGH

Perhaps more than any other, **THE HOLY BLOOD AND THE HOLY GRAIL** is responsible for the current interest in Rennes-le-Château in the English-speaking world. So for that, those of us who have read it and developed a consuming interest in all its ramifications, must forgive them for the rather large red herring it contains. In a sentence, they postulate that a dynasty of kings, tracing their lineage from King David of Israel around 1,000 BC down through Jesus of Nazareth, the Merovingians, the Plantagenets, the Houses of Anjou, Lorraine and Guise to the Hapsburg-Lorraines of the present day, maintains a divine right to rule France as well as most of the major thrones of Europe. The secret of this right has been guarded at Rennes under the historical auspices of the Knights Templar, the Cathars and the Freemasons and all controlled by a shadowy secret society called the Priory of Sion, whose current heir is Pierre Plantard St. Clair, and which spreads its web across all the influential religious, political and economic bodies of Europe and North America. The divine right is claimed on account of the supposition that Jesus did not die on the Cross, but, being of the Royal House of David, was married, probably to Mary Magdalene, had children, survived a faked crucifixion and escaped with his family ending up after many vicissitudes in the south of France. This is all tied in with legends of the Holy Grail, which in France is called *San Graal*. With a slight shift in the letters and adjusting the meaning, this becomes *Sang Réal* or *Holy Blood*. Henry Lincoln has also followed up the researches of David Wood and produced a book called THE HOLY PLACE, which investigates a giant landscape pentagram in the valley of the Aude.

LIONEL FANTHORPE

Lionel is a priest and a science fiction writer who, in **THE**

MYSTERY OE RENNES-LE-CHÂTEAU, examines the legend of Saunière as one cleric understanding another. As a writer of fantasy, he also identifies key elements of the Rennes mystery in the works of other science fiction and fantasy writers such as J.R.R. Tolkien, Isaac Asimov and Umberto Eco. He argues strongly against Rennes-le-Château concealing any heretical proof that the story of Jesus is not as it is told in the gospels of the New Testament; and that Saunière as a priest could not have held the Vatican to any kind of ransom as the Church of Rome in collusion with hypothetical vested interests, would have found far cheaper and more effective ways of dealing with him. He looks into the rumours of alchemical practices at Blanchefort and the possibility of Saunière using the Convocation of Venus to foretell the future for large sums of money. He also looks into the lives of other priests who have had some kind of connection with the mystery, in particular the abbé Boudet.

DAVID WOOD & IAN CAMPBELL

David Wood is a qualified map-maker with a keen interest in the classics and ancient legends. Applying his professional skills to the ancient churches and place names in the Aude valley, he discovered a geometric pattern of immense proportions of which Rennes-le-Château is an integral part. The basic component is the pentagram, a five pointed star, sacred in ancient religions but a symbol of the Devil and the Antichrist to the Catholic Church. He concludes that Rennes is part of a message left by visitors to the Earth hundreds of thousands of years ago when the planet was being bombarded by bodies from outer space. He connects all kinds of monuments and phenomena and the works of those apparently 'in the know' such as Nicholas Poussin, Jules Verne and the Bible, to show that mankind was genetically engineered from apes by these visitors, who based themselves on Mars as they could not cope with Earth's gravity. When catastrophe came, they all fled except for Isis and Set, who stayed behind to show mankind how to survive, and to warn, in information placed indelibly in the landscape, that the comet with strike again, possibly in our lifetime or that of our children and grandchildren. These beings are the ones we call in all languages and cultures THE GODS. In **GENISIS** he shows that all the measurements used were based on the Egyptian cubit and the English mile; and in **GENESET** that the sine of trigonometry was the key to the incredibly complicated mathematics required to set everything up. In other words, mankind will have to develop a sufficiently sophisticated degree of proficiency in mathematics in order to be able to calculate what is going to happen, when and how to survive it. Like all other researchers, he concludes that this information has been passed down in strict secrecy by a band of initiates to prevent it from being destroyed by the Catholic Church.

MICHAEL GABRIEL

This is the author for anyone with astrological interests. He is well versed in astrology and ancient lore and describes the calendrical system mapped into the landscape. In **THE HOLY VALLEY AND THE HOLY MOUNTAIN** he also shows how the cult of Woman - he has found a phenomenon he calls Microcosmic Woman (Malkuth? Ed.) - and the Great Goddess have been etched there also.

ELIZABETH VAN BUREN

In a whole series of books but most notably **REFUGE OF THE APOCALYPSE** this author takes us whole-heartedly into the realms of mysticism and alchemy. For her the gold is Light itself. Rennes-le-Château is the original Temple of Solomon, the sacred site of the Merovingians, who were descended from one of the tribes of Israel. A group of initiates including Leonardo da Vinci, Rabelais, Fulcanelli, Jules Verne and Maurice Le Blanc, have passed this information down. They have been guarding the secret of the royal descent of the one born to be the Grand Monarch at the End of the World. This secret is related to the science of Light and this is the gateway to the subterranean world where a seed group of humanity will be able to escape the devastation of the Apocalypse.

LYNN PICKNETT & CLIVE PRINCE

Having discovered in **TURIN SHROUD – IN WHOSE IMAGE?** that the first owners of an artefact known as the Shroud of Christ (although probably not the Turin Shroud itself), were the Charnay family, whose most memorable member was one of the two Templars burnt at the stake by Philippe le Bel in 1314, and who owned Rennes-le-Château at the time, Lynn and Clive then turn their researches to the secret of the Templars themselves. In **THE TEMPLAR REVELATION** starting with the mystery of Rennes-le-Château and all its various elements they discover the importance of Mary Magdalene and John the Baptist and eventually they link them with an obscure Manichean sect in the Middle East.

RICHARD ANDREWS & PAUL SCHELLENBERGER

Probably one of the most controversial books to be published on the mystery, in **THE TOMB OF GOD** Andrews and Schellenberger identify a site of tremendous importance on Pech Cardou using geometry found in the coded parchments and extrapolating that to the area with new interpretations of the features mentioned. This is then extended to conclude that the site conceals the location of the body of Jesus. The BBC Timewatch documentary team did a notorious exposé of the Andrews & Schellenberger theory, suggesting quite understandably that, since the parchments had been exposed as fakes (in fact they are modern fabrications – a slightly difference in meaning but very important) then no credence can be given to their theory. In fact since **THE TOMB OF GOD** was published a number of other researchers have been looking at Andrews & Schellenberger's work and come to some very interesting conclusions of their own.

PATRICK BYRNE

In **THE LAST SECRET OF FREEMASONRY**, published on the internet in 1999, Patrick Byrne, a Freemason of 30 years standing, has come to conclusion that a treasure of immense spiritual importance was buried by the Templars on Pech Cardou, not far from Rennes-le-Château. This was to be the centre of their new Jerusalem where they had concealed the Ark of the Covenant in a new Temple deep within the mountain.

BILL KERSEY

Two of the most enduring puzzles in the Rennes mystery are the identity, in the large parchment, of the key guarded by Poussin and Teniers and the meaning of 'blue apples.' In his book **STILL SPINS THE SPIDER OF RENNES-LE-CHÂTEAU** Bill Kersey sets out the result of his researches into the Rennes mystery, based basically on Gérard de Sède's book, **L'OR DE RENNES,** and the parchments and has come up with some very interesting and original ideas. He produces a geometric figure, based on the square progressed by the Golden Mean which he says is known in Greek as a *helix pommata*, translated as 'blue apple' using a pun (an essential element of he language of the Rennes mystery) and which he has found underpinning virtually all the important images in the mystery. He also manages to produce the only real evidence that I personally have seen linking the landscape of Poussin's *Les Bergers d'Arcadie* with the landscape of the Rennes area and for that alone this book is worth reading.

FRENCH AUTHORS

There are over 200 books published in French devoted to the mystery of Rennes-le-Château written from a wide variety of perspectives. However, the authors mentioned here have all written books based on original archives and documents associated directly with Bérenger Saunière and these are the books to read to get a more comprehensible picture based on the evidence. Unfortunately, only two of them have had any work published in English. These are Gerard de Sede's **THE GOLD OF RENNES,** translated and published by Bill Kersey, and Andre Douzet's SAUNIÈRE**'S MODEL AND THE SECRET OF RENNES-LE-CHÂTEAU,** which uses my translation of **NOUVELLES LUMIERES SUR RENNES-LE-CHÂTEAU** by Antoine Bruzeau and Benoit Riviere and is published by Adventures Unlimited.

CLAIRE CORBU & ANOINE CAPTIER

Claire Corbu is the daughter of Noël Corbu, and Antoine Captier is the grandson of the bell-ringer, who made the discovery in the old balustrade. In **L'HÉRITAGE DE L'ABBÉ SAUNIÈRE** they have published their conclusions about the source of his wealth according to his own daily notebooks, receipts, invoices, etc., that were found in a box in Marie Denarnaud's room after her death.

RENÉ DESCADEILLAS

An eminent member of the Society for the Scientific Study of the Aude and a meticulous researcher, he was a respected authority on the history of the region until his death in 1986. In **RENNES ET SES DERNIERS SEIGNEURS**, he traces the history of the Lords of Rennes, and in **LA MYTHOLOGIE DU TRÉSOR DE RENNES**, he examines the history of abbé Saunière and puts the works of many of the authors responsible for the interest in the abbé's affairs under the historical microscope. He draws his conclusions in a rational and objective fashion and his are the works to consult if you want the facts.

JACQUES RIVIÈRE

In **LE FABULEUX TRESOR DE RENNES-LE-CHÂTEAU**, Jacques Rivière looks at abbé Saunière, particularly his lawsuit, in the light of the documents relating to his case held in the archives of the bishop of Carcassonne. He sees Saunière as wanting to turn Rennes-le-Château into a place of pilgrimage and his estate as a place from where he would preach his message. He was a man with a dream who never lived to see it fulfilled.

PIERRE JARNAC

In his two volumes, **HISTOIRE DU TRÉSOR DE**

RENNES-LE-CHÂTEAU and **LES ARCHIVES DU TRÉSOR DE RENNES-LE-CHÂTEAU**, Pierre Jarnac gives a fully comprehensive account of Rennes-le-Château, Abbé Saunière and the treasure. The *Histoire* is a condensed history of Rennes-le-Château and the surrounding districts from earliest times to the 1960s and 70s. Volume One of the Archives is devoted to the mystery as it unfolded through the press from 1956. Volume Two has pen portraits, cameos and concise accounts of all the peripheral people and artefacts and the various writers on the subject He also publishes three booklets called **MÉLANGES SULFUREUX**, which contains the documents relating to the Priory of Sion from the Dossiers Secrets in the Bibliothèque Nationale in Paris. These are known as the Priory Documents.

GERARD DE SEDE

Numerous works on the historical and esoteric matters but especially **L'OR DE RENNES**, which told the original tale of Abbé Saunière, picked up by Henry Lincoln and which is at the heart of most of this book. This is now available in English as **THE GOLD OF RENNES**, translated and published by Bill Kersey.

ANTOINE BRUZEAU & BENOÎT RIVIÈRE

Two relative newcomers to the area of published work on Abbé Saunière and the Rennes mystery although they have been researching the mystery of Abbé Saunière for many years.. They have discovered that our priest led a secret life not in Paris but in Lyon. This is discussed in **NOUVELLE LUMIÈRES SUR (NEW INSIGHTS INTO) RENNES-LE-CHÂTEAU**. This book appears in English included in **SAUNIÈRE'S MODEL AND THE SECRET OF RENNES-LE-CHÂTEAU**.

ANDRE DOUZET

Part of the team that discovered abbé Saunière's secret life in Lyon, he is now writing a series of books based on his researches, the current one being **SAUNIÈRE'S MODEL**

AND THE SECRET OF RENNES-LE-CHÂTEAU in which he details his researches into the maquette and the connections he has found between abbé Saunière and the Opoul-Perillos area near Durban in the Corbières.

JOS BERTAULET
Not a Frenchman but a Dutchman who, in **DE VERLOREN KONING EN DE BRONNEN VAN DE GRAALLEGENDE,** relates how he has found a tomb at Notre Dame de Marceille using Boudet's **LA VRAIE LANGUE CELTIQUE ET LE CROMLECH DE RENNES-LES-BAINS.** Again, this is not available in English yet, but I believe that plans to translate it are under way.

There are huge numbers of works published both between the covers and on the internet and in many languages now. There are even computer games based on the Rennes mystery and the main characters. However, the reliability of the information contained in them depends entirely on the motives of the authors and their backers. The authors mentioned here are those English ones who have been most influential in publicising the mystery for whatever reason, and the French ones who have investigated the stories as told by Noël Corbu and Gérard de Sède and published their findings, along with their conclusions, backed up in the main by primary source material.

BIBLIOGRAPHY

My special thanks go to:
- JENNY BARKWAY for her article on Marie de Nègre d'Ables in the Rennes Group Newsletter October 1992.
- NICOLE DAWE for her article on Abbé Boudet in **'Le Reflet'** Autumn 1994
- VALERIE MARTIN B.A. for her article on Saint Sulpice in the Rennes Group Newsletter February 1993
- MARKE PAWSON for his manuscript **THE GOLDEN THREAD** (as yet unpublished)
- PAUL SMITH for his **'Mystical Chronologies Third Edition Revised 1994',** his invaluable information on the Priory of Sion and for the many other snippets of his meticulous research which he is kind enough to send me.
- PETER O'REILLY for his dogged research on the *Hiéron du Val d'Or*
- various **RENNES GROUP NEWSLETTERS** & **RENNES-LE-CHÂTEAU OBSERVER.**
- Pierre Jarnac and **PEGASE**, the French magazine devoted to the Rennes mystery, published by.
- Patrick Mensior, for making Noel Corbu's unpublished manuscript available to me and for many other snippets of information.
- Sandy Hamblett and **THE JOURNAL OF THE RENNES ALCHEMIST**, for the invaluable research she is doing into the origins of Godefroy de Bouillon and the Knights Templar.

BOOKS SPECIFICALLY ABOUT THE RENNES MYSTERY

MICHAEL BAIGENT. HENRY LINCOLN & RICHARD LEIGH, The Holy Blood and the Holy Grail, (Jonathan Cape Ltd. 1982)

HENRI BOUDET, La Vraie Langue Celtique et le Cromlech de Rennes-les-Bains, (Bélisane 1984)

CLAIRE CORBU & ANTOINE CAPTIER, L'Héritage de l'Abbé Saunière (Bélisane 1985)

114

RENÉ DESCADEILLAS, Mythologie du Trésor de Rennes (Editions Collot 1991)

ANDRE DOUZET, Rennes-le-Château and Saunière's Model (Adventures Unlimited 2004)

LIONEL FANTHORPE, Rennes-le-Château, (Bellevue Books 1991)

PIERRE JARNAC, Histoire du Trésor de Rennes-le-Château (L'Association pour le développement de la lecture, 1984)

PIERRE JARNAC, Les Archives de Rennes-le-Château, vols. I & 2, (Belisane 1987 & 1988)

PIERRE JARNAC, Mélanges Sulfureux (C.E.R.T. et Pierre Jarnac, 1994)

HENRY L.INCOLN, The Holy Place (Jonathan Cape Ltd. 1991)

JACQUES RIVIÈRE, Le Fabuleux Trésor de Rennes-le-Château, (Bélisane 1995)

BÉRENGER SAUNIÈRE, Mon Enseignement A Antugnac 1890 (Bélisane 1984)

ELIZABETH VAN BUREN, The Refuge of the Apocalypse (The C.W. Daniel Company Ltd. 1986)

DAVID WOOD, Genisis (Baton Press 1985)

DAVID & IAN CAMPBELL, Geneset (Bellevue Books 1994)

DAVID WOOD & IAN CAMPBELL, Poussin's Secret (Genisis Trading Co. Ltd. 1995)

RICHARD ANDREWS & PAUL SCHELLENBERGER, The Tomb of God (Little, Brown & Co. 1996)

LYNN PICKNETT & CLIVE PRINCE, The Templar Revelation (Bantam Press 1997)

GUY PATTON & ROBIN MACKNESS, Web of Gold (Sidgwick & Jackson 2000)

GENERAL BIBLIOGRAPHY

CHRIS BARBER & JOHN GODFREY WILLIAMS, The Ancient Stones of Wales Blorenge Books 198g)

THE BIBLE

ROSALIND & CHRISTOPHER BROOKE, Popular Religion in the Middle Ages (Thames & Hudson 1984)

EDWARD BURMAN, The Templars

DISCOVERING THE GREAT PAINTERS - POUSSIN, (Fabbri Publishing UK Ltd 1992)

MALCOLM GODWINSON, The Holy Grail (1994)

ROBERT GRAVES, The Greek Myths (Penguin 1955)

ROBERT GRAVES, The White Goddess (Faber & Faber 1961)

SUSAN HASKINS, Mary Magdalene (Harper Collins 1994)

DONOVAN JOYCE, The Jesus Scroll (London 1975)

MARK KURLANSKY, Salt, A World History (Jonathan Cape 2002)

LAROUSSE ENCYCLOPAEDIA OF WINE (1994)

THE ENCYCLOPAEDIA OF MAN, MYTH & MAGIC (Purnell 1970)

OXFORD DICTIONARY OF THE CLASSICAL WORLD

ELAINE PAGELS, The Gnostic Gospels (London 1980)

YURI STOYANOV The Hidden Tradition (Arkana 1994)

MICHAEL WOOD, In Search of the Trojan War.

'Les Bergers d'Arcadie' by Nicholas Poussin   [Louvre]

Saunière's Maquette

Bas-relief of Mary Magdalene on the front of the main altar in the
church at Rennes-le-Château.

Aerial view of Rennes-le-Château.
(Artist unknown)

Abbé Berenger Saunière

Church of St Mary Magdalene at Rennes-le-Château.

La Tour Magdala

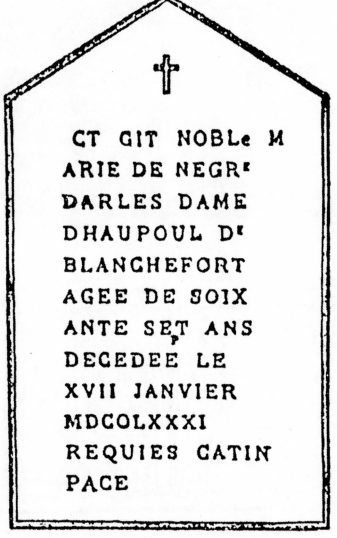

Stele (upright tombstone) of Marie de Nègre d'Ables

Dalle de chevalier

Line drawing of the 'dalle de chevalier', said in the Dossiers Secrets to depict the flight of Dagobert II's son, Sigebert, to the Razés following his father's assassination at Stenay in Austrasia.

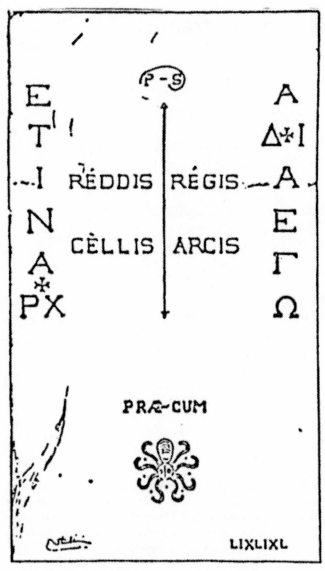

Dalle (horizontal tombstone) of Marie de Nègre d'Ables.

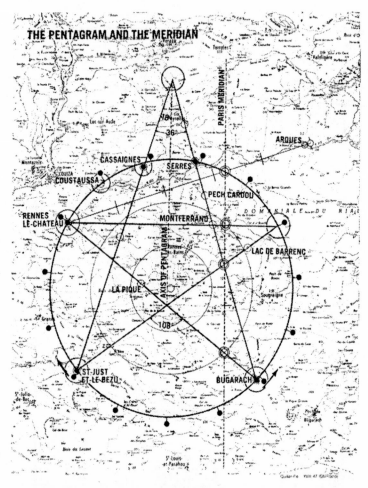

The giant pentagram found in the landscape by David Wood. This is part of a very intricate pattern of geometry using markers which are said to be far older than the post-Crucifiction, or Gothic markers of the Tomb of God, or Templar geometry. It has a totally different, quite unrelated, significance.

LA VRAIE

LANGUE CELTIQUE

ET

Le Cromleck de Rennes-les-Bains

PAR

l'Abbé H. BOUDET

CURÉ DE RENNES-LES-BAINS (AUDE)

CARCASSONNE

IMPRIMERIE FRANÇOIS POMIES, RUE DE LA MAIRIE, 50

JESVS(VRGOANTC(J(KATP(SPASCShL(V(NJTTb(Tb9aNraMVRaT
JV(RLOTILZa•VVJMOKTYVVJ9V(MMSVJCTYTAVITIY(SVJF(a((RVNT
LAVI(M•TT(a(NaPMTbT(TOMaRThAh(MINIJTRRabLT(bLSLRVJO
V(ROVNXVJ(RaTT(•dTSCOV(M(NTdTLVJCVJMMaRTaL(RGOaCb((P
TT(KTbRa(MYNNG(NTTJNaRaTPFTJTT(I9PR(TTOVJT(TVN(XTTP(
dP(STRVa(T(XT(JRJTT(aYPTIRTJHSVIJP(Pd(S(RTPT(TdO(Mb(STM
PLFT(a(JT((XVNG(TNTTOaa(R(aIXaIT(RGOVRNV(M(XdGTSCTPVhl
TJ(TVTXTVd4Xb(aRJORTIJ9VJY(RaTCVhMTRadTTTVRVJ9TVaR(hO((VN
h(N VIV(MNONXV(NVTTGR((NPaTSd(NaaRVJ(TddaTU(M(SGT(
G(NT(J?dTXTNVF((MhO((NON9VJTAd((GO(NTSP(R(RTTN(b(aT
ad(VTMS(d9Vhh(F VR((RT(T(OV(VIOSh(ab(NJ((a9VaC(MVTT(ba
'N(MTVRPOTR(ab(T(dTXTT(JRGOI(JhVJJTN(PTLLa(MVNTTXdIR(MS
(PV(GTVRa(M)S(a(S(RVN(TILL9VdPaVPJ(R(S(NhT(MJ(MPG(RhL
b(MTTJNObLTTJCV(MF(M(aVI(T(MNONS(S(MP(RhaVb(IIS(JOGNO
VILT(ROTZVRbaMV9LTa(XT(MVda(TST9VTaTLOLT((STX(TV(N(
aRVHTNONHPROT(PRT(SV(M(TaNT•M(MS(dVTLVZaRVMPVTd(R
(h•T9V((M K(VS(TaOVTTa(MORRTVTSCPOGTTaVK(RVNTahVT(MP
RVTN(TP(JJa((R(dOTVMV(MT(TLaz(aRV(MTNaT(RFT(TR(NT9
(VTa(MYLVTTPROP9T(RTLhXV(MahThGNT(XVGT•a(TSN(T(R(d
d(bLNTTNT(JV(M

NO P IS

JÉSV. M(d(La.VVLN(RV(M + SP(S.VNa.P(ENIT(NTIV(M).
P(R.MaGdaLaNa.La(RY(Mas + P((aTa.NOSTRa.dILVaS.

Parchment I

126

ÉTFACTVMESTEVMIN
SAbbATOSECVNdᴏPRIMO à
bIREPERSCCETESdISGIPVLIAVTEMILLIRISCOE
PERVNTVELLERESPICASETFRICANTESMANTbVS + MANdV
CAbANTQVIdAMAVTÉMdEFARISAEISdT
CEbANTELECCEQVIAFACIVNTdTSCIPVLITVISAb
bATIS + QVOdNONLICETRESPONdENSAVTEMINS
SÉTXTTAdEOSNVMQVAMbOC
LECISTISQVOdFECITdAVTddVANdO
ÉSVRVTIPSEÉTQVICVMEOERAI + INTROIbITINdᴏMVM
dÉIETPANESPROPOSITIONIS   REdIS
MANdVCAVITÉTdEdITETQVI   bIES
CVMERANTUXÿᴏ QVIbVSNO
NᴜICEbATMANdVCARESINON   SOLIS SACERdoTIbVS

℗⅁

Parchment II

Geometry found in Parchment II
by Richard Andrews and Paul Schellenberger

The Visigothic pillar in which Abbé Bigou is said to have put the parchments, and on which Abbé Saunière carved: 'MISSION 1891'

NOTE ON ILLUSTRATIONS

Where their origin is known, the illustrations in this book are reproduced by kind permission. Every effort has been taken to identify and contact copyright owners. However, if there have been any oversights or failures of attribution, please advise the publishers, who will be pleased to correct them in future editions.

Printed in the United Kingdom
by Lightning Source UK Ltd.
111535UKS00001B/4-21